KNIFE

# IFE

## TEXAS STEAKHOUSE MEALS AT HOME

### JOHN TESAR

**AND JORDAN MACKAY**

PHOTOGRAPHY BY  KEVIN MARPLE

FLATIRON
BOOKS
NEW YORK

KNIFE. Copyright © 2017 by John Tesar. All rights
reserved. Printed in the United States of America. For
information, address Flatiron Books, 175 Fifth Avenue,
New York, N.Y. 10010.

www.flatironbooks.com

All photographs copyright © 2017 by Kevin Marple

Food styling by Paige Fletcher

Book design by Jan Derevjanik

The Library of Congress Cataloging-in-Publication Data
is available upon request.

ISBN 978-1-250-07917-6 (paper over board)
ISBN 978-1-250-07918-3 (e-book)

Our books may be purchased in bulk for
promotional, educational, or business use. Please
contact your local bookseller or the Macmillan
Corporate and Premium Sales Department at
1-800-221-7945, extension 5442, or by e-mail at
MacmillanSpecialMarkets@macmillan.com.

First Edition: May 2017

10 9 8 7 6 5 4 3 2 1

*To Josh Ozersky, the world's greatest carnivore, who taught me so much and inspired my cooking with his enthusiasm and passion. I feel his loss every day.*

# CONTENTS

# INTRODUCTION

I don't know when cooking a steak became so complicated. When I was growing up—and this is probably true for you too—we didn't need to have charcoal or wood chunks or lighter fluid or a hibachi or a Big Green Egg to cook a steak, much less a sous vide machine and a water circulator. You didn't have to own a backyard or blacken your hands or dispose of dusty ashes. All you needed was a big steel pan, some oil, salt, and a piece of good meat. Some of the best steaks I ever ate were cooked this way—where the beefiest flavor and the deepest crust depended mainly on a good pan, a strong burner, and an honest piece of meat. I like to call this method Back to the Pan, because it encourages people to not get too fussy about steak.

Back to the Pan is at the heart of this book, because that concept—a simple, classic technique with an emphasis on essential ingredients—was driving me when I made my deep dive into steak in 2014 with the creation of Knife, my restaurant in Dallas. Knife was a response to the sad state of the American steakhouse, which often lacks personality, verve, and distinctiveness. More important, it usually lacks good steak, a particularly galling failure when you live in Dallas, a beef capital. I wanted to celebrate and honor meat, not exploit it.

Reinventing the steakhouse was a daunting task, requiring that I first travel across the country visiting steakhouses. I ate a lot of steak, most of it uninspired, but I also got a clear sense of what was missing.

First, I went out in search of great local beef. Then, when I wanted to transform that beef to become even beefier, I found Adam Perry Lang and Mario Batali, who helped me understand the nuances of aging meat. Last, I tried to design a menu that respects that precious meat and expresses its flavors as purely as possible with some of the flair of a chef. But the philosophy of Knife is clear: Let the product speak for itself. So I kept things mostly simple in the cooking, reaching back to my roots in classic French cookery, like Back to the Pan.

I follow the same pattern in this book. I tell my own story so you'll know where I come from. I then discuss sourcing great beef, with an emphasis on the notion that you don't need to spend a fortune to have great-tasting meat, so I introduce you to the Old School cuts—a filet is a great steak, but more often you can find even more flavor in lesser-known cuts at just a fraction of the price. In the equipment chapter, I detail just that: the few things you'll need to deliver the most perfect steaks at home. Beyond steak, *Knife* is devoted to the celebration of meaty deliciousness in every form. To that end, I back-loaded the book with the recipes and techniques to execute everything we do.

My wish is that you will create the ideal steakhouse meal at home. It's not complicated. All the tools, techniques, and, nowadays, great meat are available to you. A delicious, perfectly cooked piece of meat is a precious thing—I hope it means as much to you as it does to me.

# A KITCHEN LIFE

Mistakes happen quickly; comebacks take a long time. I've said that to myself more than once over my career, as those sentiments ring painfully true in both the kitchen and in life. Over and over, I've tumbled from the tops of mountains that took me years to climb. And each time, I've made the long, laborious ascent back to the summit.

My latest campaign has been the steakhouse and American beef. How a New York chef came to Texas, much less how I came to own a steakhouse in Dallas, is a piece of a much longer culinary tale. It's a story with many generous spoonfuls of success right alongside several heaping servings of failure. I want to tell a little bit of my story not out of vanity—to be sure, this tale often doesn't flatter me—but to describe how a chef develops, how a surplus of manic energy can be defused through the kitchen, and how acquiring a foundation in the basic elements of cooking can help you lead a rich life. I also want you to understand me so that you can ultimately see what Texas, Texas beef, and serving steak in America mean to me. Even though you might have seen the cover of a magazine proclaiming me the "Most Hated Chef in Dallas" or watched me on *Top Chef* or read about my public dustups with the restaurant critic here in Dallas, I want you to know that what matters to me is creating beautiful food and making customers happy. Yes, I'm prone to volatility. I suppose I'm an old-school chef in that sense, but I'm also grounded in a way I've never been before in my life, thanks to Texas and thanks to beef.

One thing most people don't know about me is that every day I run. Like a frigging windup doll, I get on a treadmill and race my legs for an hour, sometimes more. I do it in the late afternoons after work—and before work continues. People ask, "Don't you tire yourself out? Aren't you already on your feet day and night?" The answer is yes, I'm on my feet all day long. And, no, I don't tire myself out. The running is in fact to let off steam, to burn off the excess energy that buzzes in my mind and body every day. If I didn't run, I'd probably burst. And I've been like that my whole life. I've been running, burning energy, moving. Always moving. Sometimes to my benefit, sometimes to my detriment. But always, always moving.

I'm not sure where the energy comes from. Maybe it belongs to Thomas Kenyon. That's the name on my birth certificate. I was born to parents I never knew. I heard my biological father was an Irish gangster, but I don't know for sure. They put me up for adoption as an infant only weeks old, and I was taken in by second-generation immigrants, a Czechoslovakian couple already in middle age. My new grandparents didn't speak English, only Czech. Suddenly, I was John Tesar, the only identity I've ever known. But just as I am now a New York chef who has found his identity a long way away in the state of Texas, sometimes I wonder what the dynamic of being a kid with Irish DNA raised by strict Czechs has done to me. It must produce some amount of internal tension and energy. Most chefs have a lot of tension and a lot of energy. Probably not as much I do, though.

I grew up about as far culturally from Dallas as could be imagined in America—in the boroughs of New York City and, perhaps more significantly, on the shores of Long Island. My parents were very strict and disciplined. One major theme was work. The other was food. My mother was relentlessly in the kitchen, putting breakfast, lunch, and dinner out for, at minimum, the four of us—and for five times that when the extended family came over. So, in a way, I've always been in the restaurant business—as busboy, server, and host in my own home.

My grandmother would make the Czech food—rabbit in dill cream sauce, venison-and-potato dumplings. My aunt would make the salads and the apple pie. My mother had spent time with Italian women and made Italian food. Every Christmas Eve was the Feast of the Seven Fishes—squid, clams, fried flounder, fluke, every type of fish known to man. On the weekends at our house in the Hamptons, we would always have guests. You'd wake up, and there'd be ten people at the breakfast table, with my mother scrambling eggs and frying bacon for a small army. Every once in a while, I'd be asked to make eggs Benedict because I had shown an interest in the kitchen.

My father was a banker. Today, you think of some guy in a Brooks Brothers suit climbing out of a black car on Wall Street, but it wasn't like that. My dad was more like someone you'd see in one of those Martin Scorsese period pieces. He was a small-time banker working in Queens and never made more than $50,000 a year. Though my father wasn't Italian, several of his clients were in the mob, and they always treated him really well. Sometimes he'd come home with twenty pounds of meat they'd given him, or

cheese and olive oil, caviar and booze—stuff we couldn't afford. He had good taste, though. His favorite white wine was white Burgundy, long before it was cool.

In my early youth, I was witness to this kind of old-world kitchen—everything made from scratch every day—and as I got older I absorbed it. The first time I cooked anything by myself was at age twelve. While my mother was out running errands, I pulled down a cookbook and produced crescent cookies from scratch. When she got home, her first reaction was, "These look just like mine!" When it comes to cooking, I've always been a sponge. I'm sure I had just watched her make cookies enough times that I'd internalized the process.

It was also during this time that I had my first steak. My father worked in the Queens neighborhood of Kew Gardens, and one day, I remember he took me with him when he went to eat at a mob-owned steakhouse. He ordered a filet mignon that had been perfectly sizzled in the restaurant's gas-fired steak broiler. Its magical aroma preceded it as it came to the table— savory and beefy with a perfume of meaty deliciousness. It came out perfectly browned and juicy, and I'll never forget it. I just fell in love with meat and thus fell into a phase where all I wanted to eat were steak and lamb chops.

**THE BAY**

I had little inclination how much my life would change when my father bought a lot out on Long Island near Shinnecock Bay. Long Island, its wonderful bay, and the Hamptons would play huge roles in what I was to become. But first I learned what it meant to be bay people.

The name *Tesar* comes from *Tesach*, which in Czech means "carpenter." And my father very much lived up to his name. He was a natural

master carpenter. (He was also an incredible pianist; I think it was being so talented with his hands but relegated to a job in a suit behind a desk that drove him to drink.) I saw his woodworking side flower when we'd go to the Hamptons. First, he built our house. He also built boats, beautifully rendered wooden boats with curved sides and polished, gleaming staves. Proof of my adoption is that, though my name is Tesar, I have none of my father's talents: I can't cut a piece of wood straight to save my life.

But I can cook—and our family's cooking took a new turn as more and more of our lives revolved around the water. Our cuisine wasn't farm to table; it was bay to table. My dad worked the bay himself. A passionate fishermen, he'd often take me out with him to cast lines for flounder. He knew all the local fishermen and clammers and oystermen, and many a night, he came home with a bounty of the freshest seafood. We often had crowds on these weekends, and he'd get buckets of lobster and crab, and we'd spread newspaper over the tables and bury cases of Heineken in ice. The boys would be in the backyard shucking littlenecks and steamers. And in the fall, we'd cook scallops. At dinnertime, we'd heave twenty lobsters up on the table with french fries, sliced tomatoes, and corn on the cob.

On my thirteenth birthday, my dad bought me a surfboard, signaling a profound shift in my life, because I started to evolve from being a nerdy kid to hanging out with the surfers. This was the early '70s. Surfing culture today might mean yuppies in Patagonia fleeces getting a morning surf in before sipping on green tea soy lattes in meetings with venture capitalists. Back then, surfing was counterculture—it was edgy, nonconformist, rock and roll.

As I became a pretty proficient surfer, I discovered pot and the beach and new people. I started hanging out with the cool kids. When I turned fifteen, my parents trusted me enough to let me go out at night. At curfew, I'd run home from wherever I was—always running—because I didn't have a car.

Two friends from the beach were both cooks at this celebrated local joint, Magic's Pub, and lived in the apartment above it. They got me a job as dishwasher, the beginning of my restaurant career.

## MAGIC'S

Magic's was a legendary place in Westhampton in the '70s. Its cozy interior was furnished with reclaimed wood paneling. Oak tables were set with blue-and-white-checkered tablecloths during the day, red-and-white checkers at night. Everyone hung out at Magic's, high society and low.

When I mention the Hamptons, you must realize this was before it was *the Hamptons* of today. Back then, the Hamptons was an artist colony. Montauk was a fishing village. Manhattan's wealthy still decamped here during the summer, as they always have, but the culture was much more laid back. There was a real literary culture out there. When I worked at Magic's, Jimmy Breslin and George Plimpton would sit at the bar and talk to me while I made Bloody Marys. It was these customers and their lively, intellectual conversation that caused me to fall in love with the romance of the restaurant business. The guests were the most interesting people I could ever imagine.

Magic's menu was classic bar food, but it had purity and was cooked with heart. There was the famous Magic burger that's memorialized to this day on my menu at Knife—on a toasted English muffin with Vermont yellow cheddar cheese, applewood-smoked bacon, lettuce, tomato, and onion. There was crispy fried shrimp; the steak came with gravy made from chicken stock, Maggi sauce, and sautéed button mushrooms, and you could order french fries or a salad with it.

At first, I was the dishwasher, washing every plate by hand. The next summer, I "graduated" to putting tomato and lettuce on the plates, and I made tuna fish sandwiches at lunch. The following year, I was full-on in the kitchen—cooking steaks and burgers and starting to realize I have a pretty good touch, even with this simple food. I just instinctively knew when to flip the steaks, when to turn the heat down. I never sweated or pressed. That year, 1976, I decided to stay out in the Hamptons year round instead of going back to attend school and live in Queens. I graduated high school early at seventeen and moved in with the guys from Magic's. This time of my life still glows in my memory—working, cooking, listening to music, surfing.

As I discovered cooking—both the art of it and the simple fact of it as a job that earned me money—my life changed. The sparks that ignited America's food revolution were just starting to catch in places like San Francisco and New York. I wasn't there yet, but I knew that I enjoyed the act of feeding guests and didn't mind the long hours. My energy seemed to have no bounds. After work, we'd sometimes trek into the city, and I'd find myself at Manhattan's big-time nightclubs (disco!) until the wee hours.

## CLUB PIERRE

I worked at Magic's from 1976 to 1979. At age twenty, I left for Club Pierre, a swanky new restaurant opened by the rich New Yorker Francine Farkas, whose husband owned Alexander's department store. In the South of

France, Francine had met these two elegant chefs, Pierre and Alain, whom she brought to New York and helped get fixed up in this restaurant in the Hamptons. Their place was a major step above Magic's—classic French food rendered by real French chefs. In its heyday, to get a reservation at Club Pierre on a Friday night was next to impossible.

During the daytime, Pierre designed the menu and Alain made the pastry. Pierre cooked effortlessly, in an apron and with a cigarette balanced on his lip like Errol Flynn. At night, he never cooked. Unlike entrepreneur chefs nowadays who run to put on a chef's coat before going out on the floor to meet guests, Pierre never wore a chef's coat at night. He wore a gorgeous suit and worked the floor like a pro—always perfectly dressed, always perfectly charming. His slicked black hair and little French mustache were accessorized with Cartier, Hermès, and an eternally half-full glass of champagne.

Pierre was my original mentor. My first job at his restaurant was *garde-manger*—keeper of the pantry and preparer of cold food. I started making salads—salade Niçoise, salade verte. We tossed the Caesar salad tableside to order. The next year, I graduated to hot food. My station was the grill, the steak broiler, rack of lamb persillade, and the Dover sole.

I was loving life. At night after work, I headed to Marakesh, which was the nightclub at the time in the Hamptons, and stayed out until four in the morning. Then I'd head to the beach, where I'd sleep for a couple of hours until the sun came up. If there were waves, I'd surf until ten or eleven, take a nap on the beach, and then go to work for the rest of the day and all night. That beautiful, peaceful, eternal beach saved me. Had I worked in the city, I would have slept off

my partying in some dark hole of an apartment. In the soft sand and clean, pure light of the Hamptons, I'd be refreshed because I was in the ocean all morning.

It was Pierre who taught me how to make béarnaise sauce. As I grew more proficient, we'd spend the afternoon in the kitchen together as he walked me through the menu I'd be cooking. By the third year, I knew what to do on my own. He let me run the kitchen while he paraded through the dining room. Pierre loved my work ethic and rewarded my natural ability. I enjoyed the cooking and the positive feedback from diners. I felt my skills growing. Club Pierre, I thought, was just like getting an education in France—that is, until I went and got a real one.

## LA VARENNE

In my second year at Club Pierre, I decided to explore the epicenter of cooking, Paris. It was 1981, and I was twenty-two. Business in the Hamptons is seasonal. It dies after Labor Day, and Pierre would close the restaurant, meaning I had time to kill. My girlfriend at the time was a Yale graduate and spoke French, so we decided to venture to France together for four months. Her mother was well connected and got me an audition for La Varenne. Founded in 1975 by British-born food writer and cooking teacher Anne Willan, La Varenne was becoming renowned in the food world as an intimate, highly serious cooking school that offered accredited, professional degrees. Importantly, teaching was done in both French and English, which meant most of the students were Americans. It attracted the legends: Simone Beck, Julia Child—I met them all there. Many prominent American chefs had been students there too. Jonathan Waxman had gone through just a couple of years before I did, and I met the late Judy Rodgers of San Francisco's Zuni Café while there.

There were six or seven of us, and we were taught directly by two wonderful French chefs: Fernand Chambrette and Claude Vauget. In the morning, we executed the menu the chefs designed for us as they stood by and corrected technique. Then we'd all sit down and eat the lunch we'd just cooked with any guests who happened by. The afternoons were filled with demonstrations by real professionals like Michel Rostang. This was the first time I encountered delicacies like white truffles and foie gras. They graded us not just on skills but on our ability to execute dishes perfectly within set times—not too different from some of the challenges on *Top Chef*. I graduated by acing the final test— a full four-course meal.

This experience led to a multiyear stretch for me in which I'd travel to France at the close of the Hamptons season. Only that first year did I attend school. Afterward, I'd just travel around the country, interning at French restaurants for a week or two here or there, in between dining at Michelin-starred restaurants.

The ability and the knowledge I possess today I owe to those years in France. Theoretically, I'm in the second generation of new American chefs, but we all were inspired by the brilliance of French culinary technique and sensibility. It wasn't merely an education in the French kitchen; it was an indoctrination into a food culture we didn't have in America.

I'm one of the dying breed of chefs who went to Europe to learn. We didn't learn it second- or thirdhand or, god forbid, not learn it at all—as is the case with so many chefs I see in the States. We learned it firsthand. The chefs who did this became the ones who transported American cuisine into the present. Alfred Portale went to work for Jacques Maximin, and Larry Forgione worked at the Connaught in London; they both changed the New York dining scene. Jonathan Waxman, Jeremiah Tower, and Alice Waters went to France, and it changed the American dining scene. France may be the Old World, but people forget that it is also responsible for the birth of our modern food scene. If you really want to learn about food, travel. Travel to France.

## NEW YORK

The first summer at Club Pierre I worked garde-manger. Second summer, I was the broiler man. Third summer, I beat out the sous chef to take the chef position. By the fourth year, I ran the restaurant. And by the eighth year, I owned the place. Pierre moved back to France, and the restaurant was for sale. I took what would have been my college tuition, and I borrowed $36,000 from my father. My partner borrowed the same sum from his brother, who had made it big on Wall Street, and we were suddenly restaurateurs. I was only twenty-eight years old, and I owned the restaurant where I learned how to cook. Life was good. Knowing what I now know, I might even say *too* good.

We renamed the place Hampton Square, in homage to Joyce Goldstein's groundbreaking Square One in San Francisco, which was the buzz of the culinary world those days. In the summertime, we killed it, as usual, cooking Pierre's classics. A busy restaurant in the Hamptons can make enough money during the summer that you can just cruise the rest of the year. But I never cruised. I never stopped hustling. And I never stopped cooking and improving.

After Labor Day in the Hamptons, when everything shutters, I started going into

Manhattan to cook, where the food scene was electric. In the previous era, fine dining meant staid, formal French restaurants that were stuck in dishes of the past—duck à l'orange and the like. Now chefs were coming back from the South of France, the Rhône, and Italy, bringing new ideas, fusing together multiple cuisines from the Mediterranean. And the city was literally eating it up. A 1997 *New York Times* article by Marian Burros reflected on the era, saying that "at this time, the names of the famous chefs were on the cognoscenti's lips, their unlisted phone numbers eagerly sought by yuppies determined to sample $50 beggar's purses and $30 roast chicken. The excitement created by their restaurants—the Quilted Giraffe, Huberts, Jams and Arizona 206—was even greater than the clamor at today's places to be seen."

I ended up getting shifts at one of New York's new iconic joints. Arizona 206 was run by a chef barely older than I was, Brendan Walsh. He too had worked and traveled in France, as well as Italy and California, before he boldly introduced New Yorkers to the flavors of the American Southwest. It was eye opening to work with different flavors than ever before. Arizona 206 was my first exposure to Anaheim chiles, smoked chicken, freshwater fish. It was the first time I worked with pickling. I also had a job at the restaurant next door, and I'd work doubles all winter long between the two places, while sleeping at the house of my ninety-year-old aunt in Queens, commuting in and out (at all hours of the night) on the E train.

I was learning from the crème de la crème of New York chefs at the time. Employers loved me because I was a workhorse. Thanks to the Zen of surfing, I was also calm in the eye of the storm—an adrenaline junkie who stayed preternaturally serene during the rush. Of course,

I also bore a myriad of emotional problems that hadn't even revealed themselves, because I was too busy working my butt off and then partying until the wee hours. I also realized then that I had a particular talent in cooking, kind of like a photographic memory. I can go into restaurants and order a dish and, after seeing it and tasting it, completely intuit how to cook it myself. I learned a lot not just in the kitchen but in the dining room, seeing what other chefs were doing.

But beyond going to Manhattan for experience and inspiration, I also brought Manhattan back out to the Hamptons. All summer long we'd get mako shark, and swordfish and bluefish, and flounder and fluke and lobster, right out of our backyard. I brought this seafood into the '80s with a California overtone. Hampton Square was hopping; I played rock and roll, and we had a late-night bar scene crowded with Wall Street guys who flocked there because there were also girls and cocaine. And we were making money.

Then things started to go awry. Left to my own devices in the kitchen, I'd be fine forever. It's life outside of the kitchen that can prove tricky for me. In the third year of my ownership, I bought out my partner, who left me with $53,000 in payroll taxes. I had just gotten married, and my father-in-law bought in to become my partner, which wound up being a train wreck.

To try to get out from under those payroll taxes, I borrowed my friend's catering truck, rented equipment from his business, and catered parties during the day. I hired a friend of mine from the city to oversee the parties. Starting at six in the morning, I'd prep all the food for the parties and then still make it to Hampton Square each night to cook for our 200–250

covers. I paid off the $53,000, but it took a toll. I'd literally be snorting cocaine all day long to be able to maintain this manic schedule. I had a daughter with my wife, but after a year, we separated and divorced. I was blacklisted from my family, and I wasn't allowed to see my daughter. It was as ugly as ugly can get.

And times were changing. The business started to slow a bit. The center of Hamptons fashionability was shifting from Westhampton to East Hampton, and restaurant competition had arrived. Wall Street hitting bust at the end of the 1980s didn't help. I sold the restaurant, getting out before the whole thing crashed down on me.

## NEW YORK CITY

I lived on the little amount of cash I had gotten from the sale of Hampton Square until that money ran out and I got evicted from my apartment. I'd lost everything I built over the last ten years, including my family, my cars, my daughter, and my reputation. Even my girlfriend. So I turned my back on the Hamptons and headed into New York full-time, sleeping on a friend's floor while I tried to figure out what to do next. One good thing about being a chef is that, so long as you have a willingness to work hard and a modicum of talent, you can always get a job. I did the only thing I knew how to do—started from scratch.

It was 1990–1991, and scratch was a place called Formerly Joe's on the corner of Fourth and Tenth in the West Village—an unassuming place that catered to the neighborhood. This is where I met Anthony Bourdain, whom the owner brought in to help me cook. Bourdain was a bright young guy who loved food but had clear aspirations to be a writer. We had many great conversations in that kitchen and late into the night when we'd go out after work. I made

ends meet by doing a little private chef work.

Thanks to a stroke of good luck, I got the opportunity to become chef at a new place, the Supper Club, where a big raise in salary helped me truly get back on my feet again. This was the heyday of New York's club scene in the 1990s, and, as its name suggests, the Supper Club turned into an all-out club after its dinner service. MTV shot *Unplugged* there; the nightclub attracted models, power brokers, musicians. I brought Bourdain over to be sous chef with me, and for two years, we ran that kitchen.

Unfortunately, two of my worst restaurant memories were at the Supper Club. One was a kitchen nightmare on New Year's Eve, when the reservationists overbooked my expensive prix fixe meal and then doubled down on the misery by letting the rambunctious clubbers in too early. An unholy mess, it left the diners screaming for their food as the room became flooded with New Year's partiers. That night's level of yelling, stress, and chaos has never been rivaled in my career.

Another horrible memory is of the night we hosted the James Beard Awards Gala. I came up with this idea of doing foie gras and puff pastry. To merely say that the dish didn't work is an understatement that fails to capture the all-encompassing horror of the experience. First, it was a terrible dish. A lot of times—and I still do it to this day—I don't know exactly how to cook something and I just learn by doing it. Most of the time it works out; occasionally it doesn't. At this time, I had barely ever worked with foie gras and not since my schooling days in France. I overcooked it and didn't know how to portion it properly, so I was left trying to stuff this greasy, mushy, overcooked foie gras into puff pastry. But it wasn't just the dish; it was the audience. Not only was I making this unholy mess for the James Beard Foundation's extreme foodies, but I was flopping in front of four other accomplished chefs who were cooking the meal with me. Three worked under Daniel Boulud at Le Cirque, and the other was Laurent Manrique, a brilliant chef who grew up in Gascony, the region of France most known for foie gras, and who would go on to own his own foie ranch in California. It was like butchering "Hey Jude" in front of Paul McCartney.

Of course, I survived. And a couple of years later, after recouping my reputation as a chef, the world brought me some investors who wanted to back me in my own place.

## THE MANHATTAN ROLLER COASTER

The years between 1995, when I opened 13 Barrow Street, and 2001, when I left New York, saw some of the best and worst times of my life.

While it lasted, our little storefront in the West Village, 13 Barrow Street, was a fabulous joyride, a sustained high. We were open every day from 4:00 P.M. to 4:00 A.M. The food at 13 Barrow was in the hot style of the time—fusion. I never wanted to be labeled a fusion guy, but it was impossible not to be inspired by the likes of Jean-Georges Vongerichten, who was blowing minds at the Drake Hotel. He wasn't on the radar like he is now, but chefs were aware of what he was doing. We had a raw bar and a juice bar, and I was doing sushi and sesame noodles and California fusion pizzas—we had tandoori chicken with mango-fig chutney pizza and Peking duck pizza. Such dishes might sound odd today, but they had their own internal logic. After all, it's not too big a stretch to go from naan or a fluffy Chinese bun to pizza crust. The dishes were addictive and just what people wanted for a late-night meal. Food industry folks flocked to our ongoing late-night party. I remember one night after we received a rave from *New York* magazine, in our little forty-nine-seat space we had the entire Sirio Maccioni family at one table, Tom Colicchio at another, Bobby Flay at yet another, and Anthony Bourdain all in the house at the same time. And the bar was packed with Wall Street moguls. Another night, during a blizzard that had shut down the town, I remember sitting at the bar drinking and talking with Uma Thurman and Sarah Jessica Parker as the city sat silent under the snow.

In that review, Gael Greene wrote of me, "In a town that is bursting with kitchen talent, it's still a thrill to discover a player hurtling to a new high." She was spot on with everything, including the high. That I was able to cook from 2:00 P.M. to 4:00 A.M. every day while entertaining crowds and hanging out with fellow chefs at the end of the night was thanks to regular infusions of alcohol, cocaine, and pot. I worked while on those substances. Far from a way for me to escape, they helped me engage and focus in the eye of the storm.

Needless to say, 13 Barrow Street imploded, thanks to hidden fees, unscrupulous and inept financial partners, and my own fiscal bungling. When it ended, I cleaned up and went sober.

After this, my boom-and-bust cycle would continue. I had, as Bourdain described it in his essay collection *Medium Raw*, "a striking tendency among people I've liked to sabotage themselves." He also called me "probably the single most talented chef I ever worked with," before accurately noting that I "pretty much wrote the book on this behavior pattern: finding a way to [mess] up badly whenever success threatens, accompanied by a countervailing ability to bounce back again and again—or at the very least, survive."

Once again, I revived myself by becoming chef of another bizarre restaurant-meets-dance-club called Hush. I served delicious, creative food in the early part of the night, and then by ten thirty, the place was a thumping dance club. Another rave about my food from *New York* magazine made the experience rewarding, and I found my footing again for a couple of years, which led me to Vine, a big, high-profile, ambitious restaurant down in the Wall Street area to be opened by some megawealthy developers. It seemed like a good opportunity at the time, a natural progression into a more serious, high-profile restaurant.

I'll cut to the chase. In my career I've had multiple *New York* magazine reviews, all stellar. I've been reviewed in *The New York Times*, always positively except for a single one-star review. The one-star review devastated my life, and it was for Vine.

This was the year 2000, and a new cadre of chefs was reinventing food in New York City, supported by the critical pen of Bill Grimes at the *Times*. Grimes had identified the new style of restaurant in a different review, writing that "the outlines of the trend are not clear yet, and I'm not sure what name to give it, but there's something afoot on the dining scene . . . a number of talented chefs with strong resumes have chosen a quiet career path, opening small restaurants where everything is modest except the ambitions of the kitchen." We had a critic that was heralding change, and Vine didn't match the model he favored. In the Vine review, Grimes didn't exactly hack me to bits. It was worse than that: He bled me out slowly with thin, morbid cuts. "The food is quite decent, in a middle-of-the-road, easy-listening sort of way," he wrote.

*No one is going to stop in midsentence and exclaim over it. But no one is going to complain, either.*

*In just about any American city of half a million or fewer inhabitants, Vine would automatically be the best place in town.*

*Here, it merges into the crowd.*

In case you might have thought otherwise, chefs take reviews very seriously. *Easy listening*—he compared my food to Muzak! I've never forgotten that, and my reaction to the bad review was so powerful as to be almost cliché. I couldn't get off the couch. So faint was the praise in the review that the end for me was a foregone conclusion. One day, I walked into the office of the director of operations and caught him interviewing the new chef.

After losing my job, it took me a while before I felt like showing my face in public again. When I finally reemerged, I'd spend my days biking on the waterfront. Filled with angst and anger, I'd ride around the West Side, distracting myself from the pain.

One day in Hell's Kitchen at the intersection of Forty-Fourth Street and Tenth Avenue, I paused to look at what appeared to be the construction of a restaurant from an old gas station. As I was peering in the window, this guy from inside walked up to me and made conversation.

"So what do you do?"

"I'm a chef."

"Oh, really? We're opening our first restaurant," he said with a beginner's enthusiasm.

He asked where I worked. I told him a little about my situation and asked if they were looking for a chef.

He said, "We sort of have one already, but tell me about yourself."

So I told him, and he was impressed enough to ask for my phone number.

Not terribly long after, he called me. "Why don't you come talk to my partner, Bruce?"

I talked to Bruce, and later we did a tasting. They loved my food, and at this point, I was just looking to hide out and work anonymously somewhere no one would find me.

The restaurant, called 44 & X Hell's Kitchen, still exists today. Back then, it turned out to be just what I needed. I found my groove cooking every night for a new set of people, in a new corner of the city with an entirely different culture and population. The place started hot—all these Broadway entertainers frequented us. I remember Nathan Lane often holding court at the bar. (Broadway guys were party animals.) We got a positive nod from the *Times* and three stars from the *Daily News*, and *New York* magazine gave us an enthusiastic shout. I helped build this wonderful little joint out of nothing right after the worst failure of my life, and it felt great. I just put my head down and worked, tried to live a more balanced life. Then came 9/11, and I decided I needed to get the hell out of New York.

## WEST

And get out I did, almost as far as one can go. I took a job running multiple restaurants at a ritzy new development at Northstar in Lake Tahoe. I gave up my sublet in Manhattan, bought a Ford Explorer, got a dog, and lived the good life in Tahoe for three years. What can I say? It was a welcome respite from the nonstop grind of New York. Not that we didn't work hard. But the surfer boy in me loved the fact that I also got in 120 days a year on the slopes.

But, as they always do, things ran their course. After three quiet years, I guess the universe decided I'd had enough snowboarding, pot smoking, and hanging out with twentysomethings. One day, my fishmonger called and said, "Are you ready to come back to reality soon? Because Rick Moonen just got a deal in Las Vegas and needs a chef to run RM Seafood in New York."

Rick and I kind of knew each other, so I flew to Vegas to meet him. We hit it off, and he offered me the job. The caveat was that I had to move back to New York that week. I said, "What the hell," and embraced the change that was being thrust at me. It was upsetting to have to give my white Lab to my neighbor, but leaving all my stuff behind was liberating.

The next thing I knew, I was subletting a place on East Twelfth and Third Avenue. Soon enough I was hustling lunch and dinner out the window at RM Seafood six days a week. I became Rick Moonen while the real RM went out to Vegas to build his kingly restaurant.

But before too long, I was needed to help shore up the Vegas restaurant, so I started an insane schedule of working half the week in Vegas and then flying back to work half the week in New York. From the reputation I gained as chef de cuisine for Rick Moonen, I got the call from headhunters looking to find a chef to replace the legend Dean Fearing, longtime chef of what many considered Texas's finest restaurant, the Mansion on Turtle Creek in Dallas.

## TEXAS

I'd never been to Texas. Moving there had never even crossed my mind. But I was ready to shake up my life again. Ready for the wild ride to continue with a twist I could have never foretold. And continue it did.

I've taken over for a few people in my time, but those experiences were nothing like following Dean Fearing when he decided to move on. Coming for this job to Big D, as they call

it here, was like flying into town on a magic carpet. My arrival was a big deal; I was ushered into Dallas high society like I was a movie star. While I relished receiving praise for my craft, I'd never enjoyed much of the limelight, as the kitchen occupied so much of my time. All the attention I received changed my life, and I didn't quite know how to handle it. Dallas, as you might imagine, has quite a different dynamic from New York. And being chef at the Mansion, the dear old Cougar Palace, was an insane place to try to comprehend Dallas. The Mansion was as fussy and traditional and wild and idiosyncratic as Texas itself. I was encouraged to stay out late, throw parties, and meet people, because it brought attention to the property. They wanted me to be like Dean, because, well, Dean was—and will always be—the man.

But it's hard to think of two people with more different styles than Dean and I. I had to try to learn something of that whole Southern hospitality. Dean relishes striding through the dining room, shaking hands and kissing babies like the chef royalty that he is. And the people of Dallas absolutely love such a parade. You have to be a personality here in Texas, which is a lesson (and a skill) that has taken me time to learn, if I've learned it at all. To this day, I certainly don't behave much like a Texan, though I understand the game much better.

At the end of the day, however, you can be the most famous chef in the world, but it's really about what you put on the plate. And that's one thing Dean and I have in common. We cook. I was very proud to carry on the Mansion's tradition.

## THE MOST HATED CHEF IN DALLAS

I earned the title "Most Hated Chef in Dallas" in a *D Magazine* profile that came out after I left the Mansion two years after I started. The title was deliberately provocative, but the article didn't paint me in a bad light. Rather, it detailed a few of the scuffles I had gotten into and talked to some rival restaurateurs who didn't like me (and some who did). Like they say, you can take the kid out of New York . . . Let's just say it took a while to get used to the kitchen culture of Dallas, and I was happy to move on to pursue my own thing upon leaving the Mansion. Certainly, I had ruffled some feathers in Dallas, made some enemies. But I'd also made lifelong friends. Most important, I learned not to give a crap about what other people thought of me. My personal journey to get to this point had led me through enough twists and turns that I wasn't going to sweat the attention— good or bad. Indeed, as Oscar Wilde wisely stated, "There is only one thing in life worse than being talked about, and that is not being talked about."

But no matter whether the attention's good or bad, it's crucial to both the mind and the soul to have one person who believes in you unconditionally. Not long after I moved to Texas as chef of the Mansion, I found myself down in Austin cooking at the Hill Country Food and Wine Festival (may it rest in peace). While there I happened to meet a pastry chef from the Driskill Hotel, someone who would change my life. Tracy and I hit it off immediately; from the beginning, we had a depth of personal conversation that I rarely found even in people I'd known for decades. I had a girlfriend at the time, but Tracy and I stayed in touch. Ultimately, one thing led to another, we started seeing each other, and after I left the Mansion, we got married.

I had no idea at the time how significant this relationship would end up being for me on multiple levels. This was years before I got into beef, before I ever conceived of Knife. Tracy's family were cattle ranchers in Texas and had been for over a century. She's the child who flew the coop; the rest of them still live in the small town of Stephenville. My brother-in-law runs the family ranch. My sister-in-law is an expert in animal husbandry (she studied with Temple Grandin, the renowned animal scientist who revolutionized the slaughterhouse, making it more humane) and married another rancher with massive holdings in South Texas. Every holiday and on many weekends, we'd visit the ranch, and I learned more from this family about cattle and the beef industry than I ever thought I could. In 2010, Tracy and I had a son, Ryder. For once, my personal life was grounded, even if professionally I was still trying to discover my niche.

After the Mansion, I drifted for a while in the vapor of a couple of hasty decisions—back to New York for a few months into a booby-trapped situation, to Houston and into another one—but nothing felt right or was seemingly destined to succeed. I even went on *Top Chef* just to challenge myself and do something different—that experience is a book of stories entirely of itself. Suffice it to say that doing the show was a great, terrible, life-changing decision that I don't regret making at all. I succeeded on the show, and it served me well. That's why, despite the torture, I agreed to go back and do it again in 2016.

Upon coming back to Dallas, I realized that this was the place I needed to be. For better or worse, it had reluctantly accepted me, and I it. I'd accomplished a lot. But I could also ask myself, what had I accomplished? I'd cooked for others. I'd stood in for Rick Moonen. I'd followed Dean Fearing in a restaurant and institution that was bigger than both of us. What had I done that expressed me? Who was I as a chef?

I first attempted to answer that with Spoon. Spoon was a very personal venture, a high-end restaurant devoted to fish in the middle of northern Texas cattle country. But in emphasizing fish, I was playing against Dallas's beef-obsessed flow while paying homage to chefs I admired and from whom I'd learned a great deal—Eric Ripert and Rick Moonen. More personally, I was tracing a path back to my earliest days of cooking, eating, and living off Shinnecock Bay with my family.

Against all odds, Spoon was a hit in Dallas and beyond. It got great reviews and made *Esquire*'s ten best new restaurants list. I was bringing in some of the world's greatest product—uni, oysters, geoducks, king and Dungeness crab, spiny lobsters—and it was beautiful. I was so proud of the food we were doing there. And despite the fact that business was good, Spoon ended up closing because of shaky finances.

Even before Spoon had officially closed, we had already opened up Knife across town. And I knew Knife was going to work. Just as Spoon's seafood had captured the essence of my youth on the water, Knife was a bridge between that first memorable bite of steak I had with my father and my adopted state of Texas, where after years of searching, I feel I have finally found myself. As lovingly articulated in the rest of this book, this is Knife.

BEEF

Not all meat is created equal.

The number-one secret to making a brilliant steak is to start with high-quality meat. Yes, this meat is more expensive. (It costs more at the wholesale level for the restaurant too—we buy some of the most expensive meat out there.) But some things are more than worth the price.

There are a few truths behind the noble mantra—eat only great meat—and they're all related. First and foremost, great meat tastes better. What's the point of eating animal flesh if it has little to no flavor? Sadly, that's the state of most of the commodity chicken, pork, and beef you find at the supermarket. Bland meat needs enhancement with marinades, rubs, and sauces. There's nothing wrong with these flavor boosts, but the thing about good meat is that when you have it, you don't need anything beyond a little salt and pepper. The taste is so primal and perfect that it defies descriptive language, except as a deep, powerful "beefiness." The flavor sits somewhere amid earthy and funky, sweet and savory, but communicates a sense of stirring, deeply fulfilling umami (the fifth taste, a.k.a. the taste of protein deliciousness).

Finally, beyond flavor and nutrition, properly raised beef is important for the environment, for the health and integrity of the animals themselves, and for the people raising them, and things must be done right—humanely, generously, compassionately. Everything about raising a cow well contributes to the values of eating it—both the values we can savor and the virtues of eating something that was raised in harmony with nature.

The point I'm making is—eat better meat. Maybe eat a little less meat, but spend more on it—you will be happier and healthier. In this day and age, it's not so hard to do.

If you're fortunate to have a good butcher in your town, ask about where the meat is sourced. Butcher shops had all but disappeared for decades, but they seem to be gently rebounding as more and more people are becoming particular about their meat. If the source is good, the butcher will be more than happy to tell you about it. And nowadays, specialty grocers and even high-end stores like Whole Foods are making an effort to stock good-quality, ethically raised meat. If you're curious about the source and nature of the meat, ask the employees at the store's meat counter. If they have good product, they'll be happy to tell you about it. If you don't have access to a butcher, there are now plenty of ranchers that will gladly ship you high-quality steaks. Yes, mail-ordering adds to the cost and makes having an already spendy steak even more of an investment. But I promise you, it's worth it. And there's another way to lower the cost. Not every steak you eat needs to be a rib eye or a filet mignon. You can always save money by learning about what I call the New School cuts—delicious, relatively inexpensive cuts that are packed with flavor and come at a fraction of the cost of major cuts.

# 44
# FARMS

Please forgive the spiritual language, but the way I look at my current situation bears some kind of resemblance to this: After years of wandering in the desert, the lord above first brought me to Texas and changed my situation; then he brought me 44 Farms and changed my life.

This book is all about cooking great steak, and I offer many ideas to that end. But the first and most important requirement in producing superior steak is to start with superior meat. The supplier of most of the beef I use at Knife and my guru in all things meat is 44 Farms, a ranch in Cameron (in east central Texas, close to the middle of a triangle drawn from Dallas to Houston to San Antonio).

One of the maxims at 44 Farms is "Know Your Rancher"—a sentiment I believe whole-heartedly—so let me explain a little bit about them and why they're so important to Knife and to ranching in Texas in general.

44 Farms is family owned and operated by Bob McClaren, along with his mother, sister, and brother-in-law. But the commercial history of the farm goes back to 1909, when Bob's ancestors started in agriculture in the rich soils and rolling green hills near Cameron. When they took over, Bob and his sister decided to convert the farm into a cattle ranch and figured that the kind of cattle they wanted to raise was Black Angus, the most common breed of beef cattle in the country. At the time, Black Angus was uncommon in Texas, as the breed is considered better adapted to northern climates (it originates in Scotland). But Bob wanted to prove that well-cared-for Black Angus could flourish in Texas, so he

started his herd with the very best Black Angus specimens he could find. The rest is history. He was able to show that with proper management, Black Angus can indeed flourish in Texas, especially in the open grasslands of 44 Farms. The cattle eat grass there, as well as fermented sorghum and cottonseed, and silage, most of which is grown on the property. I'm convinced it's the cottonseed, which the cattle consume instead of hay in the wintertime, that ends up making the beef taste so good.

Primarily, 44 Farms is what's called a seed stock operation. That means they put a huge amount of effort into culling the genes of the herd to produce better and better cattle, which they then sell to other ranchers who want similarly to improve the genetics of their own herds. But, proud of the quality he was producing, Bob also decided to create a business to sell his beef on the mass market, something few ranchers do. For 44 Farms, though, selling the beef is also the best way to ensure its quality. To handle raising cattle and selling meat requires diverse skills, lots of coordination, and a great deal of effort, but the product is better and the profit is too.

In 2012, Bob started marketing their meat directly to consumers online at 44 Steaks. But along the way, a new crop of chefs in search of high-quality local product discovered 44 Farms beef. I was introduced to it by the outstanding chef Chris Shepherd of Underbelly in Houston, and it's been love at first taste. The beef is undeniably great—it has that primal resonant beefy flavor, exquisite marbling, and a beautifully juicy burst of meaty joy when you bite into it.

As good as the steaks are, the hamburger meat they produce is some of the best you can find. In the age when inspection of industrial hamburger can show that the meat composing the single hamburger sitting in front of you came from multiple continents and contains god-knows-what parts of the cow, you want to know where your meat comes from. That's why I use 44 Farms ground beef in the program I like to call One Burger, One Cow. My ground beef is not coming from different cows in different parts of the world whose various muscles and other parts are mixed together at some (or several) enormous processing plants. The beef I use comes from one place and often from one single animal.

Provenance is not only an issue with ground beef. You will have no idea where most steaks you buy at the store come from. It could be Kansas, Montana, Texas, Colorado, who knows. You won't know who raised it or how. Buying directly from a single ranch, a single producer, solves that problem. It also, through the act of cooking and eating that meat, provides a greater connection to the land and the people who raised that animal. For me, greater connection means greater happiness.

# BREEDS OF CATTLE

When you go to the store to buy meat, you'll occasionally be faced with the choice of breeds—Black Angus, Red Angus, Wagyu. What do these terms mean?

Humans have been breeding cattle for thousands of years, just as we've been breeding roses and oranges and every other domesticated organism. Just as with any animal, each newborn calf displays a unique genetic imprint, carrying on some scrambled version of its parents' traits. Over the millennia, people have selected particular individuals of their herds to interbreed, with the hope of getting offspring that will display certain traits—or simply kept the healthier, hardier calves and sold, traded, or eaten the less successful.

All cattle are derived from an ancient ox-like species, and it's estimated that cattle are one of the first species to be successfully domesticated by man. Cattle's uses for ancient humans were likely similar to what they are today—meat, milk, and work. *Taurus* and *indicus* may sound like strains of marijuana, but they're actually the two species of cattle. *Taurus* is the European species, typically adapted to cooler climates, while the *indicus* evolved in the hot climates of Africa.

In this day and age, all those bloodlines have become concentrated into over eight hundred recognized breeds. Brahman, zebu, and Sanga are *indicus* breeds, while the more familiar Angus, Hereford, Simmental, and Charolais are *taurus*. By the way, animals like yak, buffalo, and bison are so genetically close to cattle that they

too can interbreed with cattle. The object of breeding is to favor certain characteristics, anything from increased milk production, to heat or cold resistance, to docility, to rapid growth, to meat quality—and any desirable combination of those. Within each breed, dedicated ranchers—who now keep track of the genetics in highly advanced ways—continue to pair steer and cow to produce better and better offspring, which they then sell to other ranchers or continue to breed themselves.

I tend not to get too wrapped up in carrying a multitude of breeds, preferring to focus on only a couple at Knife. This is because the meat might be subtly or greatly different from breed to breed, making things unnecessarily complicated at the restaurant.

Here's a little rundown of the breeds I use, which are, conveniently, fairly common.

### BLACK ANGUS

Angus cattle are popular among ranchers because they reach maturity on the early side and carry a lot of muscle (meat) and good marbling. They're popular among chefs and diners because, when well raised, they have terrific flavor. Originally a cool-climate breed, Angus can flourish in warmer climates too with proper care. Angus cattle were first bred in Scotland hundreds of years ago. They took hold in the United States in the late 1800s and have gone on to be the most common breed of beef cattle in this country. You will also hear about Red Angus cattle, which are no different from the Black, except in color. The United States is apparently the only country to register both as separate breeds.

## Certified Angus Beef

One thing you should know about, because you'll encounter it at the store, is the Certified Angus Beef sticker you may see on packaged meat. Certified Angus Beef is a brand created by the American Angus Association to help market its beef. The absence of a CAB sticker on a piece of beef does not mean that the meat is not Angus; it's just not Angus that has been overseen by the AAA, which works with farmers and ranchers to help them raise their cattle. If the resulting beef meets the AAA's ten specifications for marbling, tenderness, and consistency, then it can be sold as Certified Angus Beef. The organization says that only one out of every four Angus cattle passes the cut. Certifications like CAB are a fine promise of a certain level of quality, but you will not know where it came from. It could be Montana, could be Colorado, could be anywhere.

### WAGYU

This much-misunderstood breed is the source of the renowned, clichéd, and overhyped Kobe beef. Kobe beef is simply a strain of Wagyu that has been raised in Hyogo Prefecture of Japan (its capital is the city of Kobe) according to the standards of the Kobe Beef Marketing and Distribution Promotion Association. Highly prized for its flavor, tenderness, and extreme marbling, Kobe beef is not seen very often outside Japan. If you've been sold Kobe beef somewhere, it's almost certainly not this special beef from Kobe. It's much more likely Wagyu that's been raised outside of Japan and is being wrongly marketed as Kobe. It might still be fine meat, just not true Kobe beef.

*Wagyu* simply means "Japanese (*wa*) cow (*gyu*)." Modern Wagyu refers to a type of cattle that have been bred in Japan since the mid-nineteenth century when Japan's native cattle were crossbred with some imported European breeds. Today, there are four breeds of Wagyu, the most common of which is Japanese Black. The second-most common is Japanese Red. Wagyu cattle have been tightly controlled by Japan. The first specimens came into the United States in 1975. Wagyu beef in America has been crossbred with American breeds to help the cattle adapt to American conditions. Here, it doesn't have to be raised with any of the same standards as in Japan, but it still provides some amazingly tender and well-marbled meat. The thing about the extreme marbling is that the fat on Wagyu melts below human body temperature, so a piece of raw beef literally melts in your mouth. Meat like this is very expensive.

## AKAUSHI

One of the four breeds of Wagyu, Akaushi is the only one constantly represented on the menu at Knife. Known as Japanese Red Cattle, the Akaushi is extremely rare. Nowadays, it's being crossbred with Angus, which allows the cattle to flourish in the climate of Texas, and makes a nice meat that adds richness and depth to the standard Angus. For many people, it ends up being their favorite cut at Knife. It's exceptional beef, with tremendous flavor, texture, and marbling.

## HeartBrand Akaushi

At Knife, we're lucky to be close to one of the country's best sources of Akaushi beef: HeartBrand Ranch, not far from Austin. Indeed, it was never meant to be imported into the country and likely won't ever be again since the sole time in 1992, when some Texas ranchers discovered a loophole (quickly closed) in the Trade Act that allowed them to bring in some Akaushi cattle. On a 747 specially outfitted to carry them, eight cows and three bulls were flown to the States. They are the seeds for the thousands of Akaushi being raised today, all under agreement and supervision of HeartBrand (from whom you can order the meat online).

# GRASS VERSUS GRAIN

There are two conversations about grass-fed beef in America. One is the political and economic conversation concerning issues of nutrition, treatment of cattle, the environment, and land use. The conversation that we chefs have, though, is usually less high-minded and more practical. That conversation is all about flavor and consistency.

It's important to know that all cattle are grass-fed for a portion of their lives. What we call conventionally raised (grain-fed) cattle are moved to a feedlot after six months or so, where a grain diet is applied for another eight to twelve months. This allows the animals to grow faster to achieve greater weight and marbling at a younger age. Animals that remain on grass for their entire lives will grow much more slowly, meaning that they will be older at the time of slaughter, their meat will be more grassy than sweet with less marbled fat, and they will also exercise more, leading to potentially tougher meat. Grass-finished beef can be delicious, no doubt, and I've considered featuring it on the Knife menu when I find some really good stuff. But, in general, it's just not consistent enough in flavor, marbling, and tenderness to warrant being an everyday staple on our menu.

I feel that grass-fed never achieves the level of juiciness and richness you can find with grain-finished meat. There are also various methods and degrees of grain finish. Much depends on the grains the cattle are fed. If the amount of corn in the feed is kept to a minimum—at 44 Farms, cattle get a little, but also a lot of other assorted grains and things like cottonseed and sorghum, both packed with nutrition—the cows are healthier and the meat more interesting and nutritious.

I'm very open to 100 percent grass-fed and have long been in search of a provider who will give me both the quality and consistency I need. Such a producer probably exists somewhere in the high altitudes of a mountain range, where the grass is green and rich, and the cattle can enjoy a diverse diet. When such beef gets mainstream enough to ensure me a consistent supply, I will be the first in line to buy it.

# UNDERSTANDING MARBLING & BEEF GRADING

I'm of two minds on grading. On the one hand, beef with the higher grade is usually better. On the other, grading for marbling doesn't tell me a lot about the taste of the beef. Let me explain further.

At your local store's meat counter, you've likely noticed stickers on various cuts of meat—Prime, Choice, Select—with prices varying respectively. These are grades handed out by the United States Department of Agriculture, rating a cow's meat based on the percentage of intramuscular fat, or marbling. This fat is called marbling because its delicate, fine striations in the meat resemble the swirling patterns of marble. That it's distributed within the muscle is important. Intramuscular fat provides some tenderness, moistness, and flavor to the meat. It's also the hardest kind of fat to encourage, only developing in cattle after the harder fat that accumulates in the gut, under the skin, and in between the muscles. Raising cattle with high degrees of marbling depends on breed, diet, and how the animals are raised. It requires not only skill by the rancher but a significant investment of capital, hence the higher price.

Since 1926, the USDA has been grading beef. Grades are determined primarily based on marbling as well as maturity of the animal and yield. Incredibly, the whole carcass is graded for marbling just by one test—a trained and certified USDA grader looks at a cross section of the carcass between the twelfth and thirteenth ribs, at the rear of the rib eye section of the animal, where one would expect to find the most marbling. Then a grade is assigned for the whole carcass. And, largely, it works, so long as marbling is your main criteria, which for most ranchers and restaurants it is.

However, it's also important to remember that this grading is a voluntary assessment submitted to and paid for by the meat supplier. The absence of a grade on a steak doesn't mean that the steak is not a superior piece of meat. Beef from smaller ranches and farms or even independent processors may not opt to have their beef graded. This might be because of the expense, because they have nothing to gain from it (since they're likely not putting their meat out in the competitive counters of grocery stores), or because the way they raise their meat doesn't promote marbling in the same way bigger operations do. Grass-finished beef is a case in point—most of it wouldn't grade well in the USDA's system.

Another thing to remember if you're insecure about purchasing ungraded beef: Beef grading isn't rocket science. If you like to cook meat at home, chances are you've eyeballed lots of steak. You know what marbling looks like, so trust your instincts. If you're looking at a piece of ungraded rib eye that still shows substantial streaks of silky white fat threading through the meat, you're probably as good a judge as anyone that it's good meat. It's also helpful to know that within the beef grades themselves there are various levels. In the industry, graders often refer to "high prime" and "low prime" to differentiate better and worse examples of Prime beef, so there's significant wiggle room even in the grades.

I've bought Prime meat that I wouldn't grade at Prime, especially during summer or in drought conditions. If the cattle haven't gotten enough water, the meat's flavor and texture can change. I don't believe marbling equals flavor, either. It only indicates a certain tenderness and juiciness due to fat. I grade beef when I eat it. That said, here's a rundown of what you're getting from the major grades.

### PRIME

The top of the line. Prime, according to the USDA, comes from "young, well-fed beef cattle . . . has abundant marbling . . . and is excellent for dry-heat cooking such as broiling, roasting or grilling." It's going to be about 10–13 percent fat content. Only about 3 percent of cattle earn the grade of Prime, which is why historically it was generally accessible solely at high-end restaurants or steakhouses. But as the price of beef has gone up, more of it has filtered down to specialty grocers. Expect high prices but great cuts of meat.

### CHOICE

Beef rated Choice boasts about 4–10 percent fat and has marbling, but not a huge amount. More than half of all beef is graded at Choice, and it's generally what you can find at good retail stores. However, there's also more variation in this category than the others. Top-end Choice can have degrees of marbling equivalent to Prime, but the maturity of the animal (say, older) might warrant a Choice rating. At the other extreme, Choice may resemble what you'd find in Select. So use your eyes, as Choice will likely be the most available, high-quality option.

### SELECT

Reflecting around a third of the beef market, Select has only slight marbling. It does, however, have good consistency and can still be useful. Coming primarily from younger animals, Select beef can be very flavorful, just not as juicy and tender. Therefore, it's not a great option for grilling (unless you're talking about the fattiest cuts), but can be great for marinating, stewing, braising, and so on.

### STANDARD OR COMMERCIAL; UTILITY, CUTTER, AND CANNER

Typically, beef that would receive these grades won't even be labeled with these low-end ratings. Standard or Commercial beef will show up in grocery stores but is very lean and tough, fit only for slow cooking. As for Utility, Cutter, and Canner—does your dog like meat?

# KNOW YOUR CUTS OF BEEF

Few people understand and can visualize where on the animal a particular piece of meat comes from. Not everyone wants or needs to know the particularities of butchering, but at the same time, if you're interested in upping your steak game, I believe you should know a little bit about where the muscle comes from and how it was used by the animal. This understanding can inform your decisions about what method to use to cook your steak, how long, what degree of heat, and so on. For instance, the familiar saying "high on the hog" relates to the location of the cuts on an animal. The muscles high up—in cattle and in pigs—don't do very much heavy lifting but rather protect the spine and the ribs. Because they work less, the meat is much more naturally tender. These are the expensive, quick-cooking cuts like steak.

We do a fair amount of butchering at Knife, but we go through too much meat at this point to break down every animal ourselves, so we also get beef precut from 44 Farms. But when we do it ourselves, this is how we look at the animal.

# BEEF PRIMALS

Whole animals can be broken down in many ways, and butchery is quite simply the strategic breaking down of a whole animal into ever-smaller parts. Strategy becomes relevant as the butcher determines the most economical and beneficial/profitable way to subdivide the animal. This means making choices that maximize the most salable cuts while leaving little to waste. Decisions on how to break down individual animals depend on the kind and quality of the animal and the desires of the people who will be buying the meat.

A butcher starts with a side of beef (literally one half of the carcass that's been split down the spine), separating the carcass into the basic cuts or primals, as they're known in the industry. The primals of beef, from the animal's head toward the tail, are chuck, brisket, shank, rib, short plate, loin, flank, and round.

When it comes to steak, we're not very interested in the chuck, brisket, and shank from the front of the cattle and the round from the rear. The muscles that comprise these primals are heavily used and will thus be tough with connective tissue, making them better candidates for the tenderizing effects of slow cooking—stewing, braising, slow roasting, and barbecue. These cuts can be tremendously flavorful, though, so don't sell them short. The chuck also has a good deal of fat, making it excellent for ground beef. (The chuck is also the source of one "new" steak cut, the flat iron, which I discuss on page 42 in the New School section.)

Steak cuts are rich, tender pieces that can be cooked quickly without being too tough. Pretty much every major steak cut comes from the top-middle of the animal—the rib and loin primals. The rib primal gives us the meaty rib rack. When separated into individual steaks, these are rib eyes. Behind the rib primal is the loin primal. This is the Park Avenue South of beef cattle, home to the tenderloin, filet mignon, strip, porterhouse, T-bone, and sirloin steak. Underneath these two primals are the sections that comprise the cow's belly. There's the short plate primal, from which we get beef ribs (beloved by fans of barbecue and braises) and skirt steak. And there's the flank primal, which gives us two more New School cuts: the flank steak and the hanger steak. Literally bringing up the rear is the round primal, which is basically the rear leg and rump—lots of meat here, but lean and tough. This meat also lacks the collagen you find in the chuck (collagen melts away during slow cooking to become delicious gelatin), so the round is best not stewed, but roasted and thinly sliced as roast beef, for instance, for an inexpensive meal or sandwiches.

At Knife, we divide our menu into what we call Old School and New School cuts. The former are the traditional steak cuts that we all know and love, what people might call the "prime cuts." The New School category consists of the more obscure but often astonishingly flavorful steaks from less-heralded regions. Often called butcher's cuts, they were the tasty little steaks that butchers would keep for themselves while selling the expensive cuts to their affluent customers. In recent years, many of these cuts have become fashionable. We love them because they taste great but are less expensive, meaning we can accommodate customers at every price range.

# OLD SCHOOL CUTS

## RIB EYE

The favorite cut of connoisseurs, the rib eye can be served boneless or bone-in. This steak is prized for its marbling and flavor—the combination of tenderness, richness, and flavor may surpass any other cut. The inclusion of the bone is a matter of preference; some people believe it confers an added dimension of flavor. The bone also slows cooking in the surrounding meat, meaning you can have a rare section on the interior while the outer regions of the steak might be medium rare. Sometimes you'll see it referred to simply as rib steak or even cowboy rib eye or tomahawk, which denotes a flashy bone-in cut where the rib bone is left attached, to a six- to eight-inch-long naked bone. In France, this piece is known as the *côte de boeuf* and is served at a massive three- to four-inch thickness with the bone in. We serve steaks like this too at Knife, and they're meant to be shared by two people.

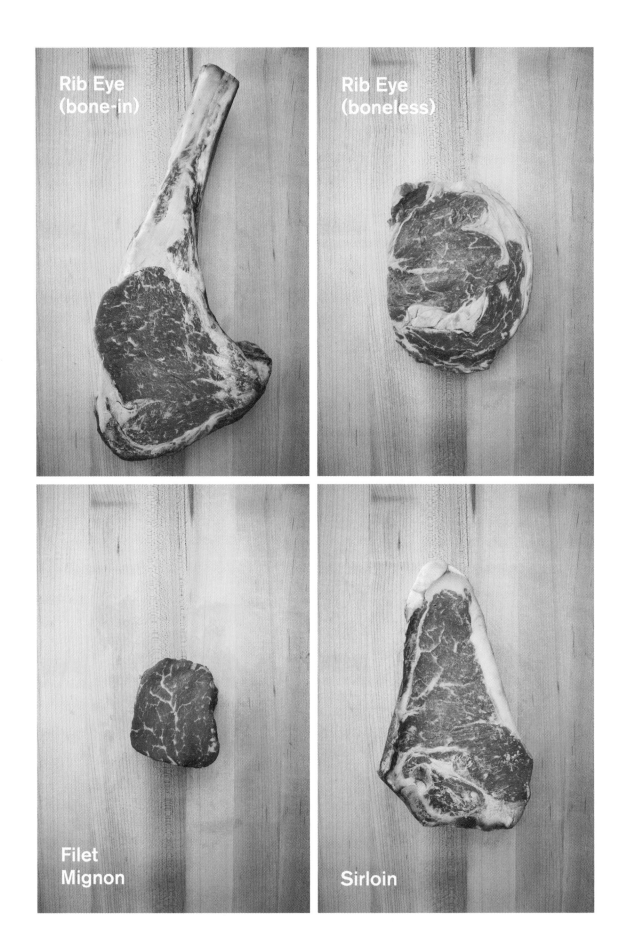

Rib Eye
(bone-in)

Rib Eye
(boneless)

Filet
Mignon

Sirloin

## The Spinalis:
## The Tastiest Morsel of a Cow

The spinalis–a.k.a. the cap steak or rib eye cap–is the most mouthwateringly tender, juicy, beefy, awesome bite of beef. It's the muscle that surrounds the rib eye's heart, separated from it by a layer of fat. On its own when cut from a single rib eye steak, it looks like a long, narrow column of meat (just an inch or so wide) that resembles a skirt. Because cows have gotten so big these days, often when you see rib eye served, the spinalis is removed, leaving just the eye, which is about as big as most people want to eat. But we leave the spinalis on to honor the cow and to reward our diners who order the rib eye. With exquisite marbling, the spinalis is impressively tender and juicy. And it achieves this without sacrificing its flavor, which is among the beefiest tastes of the cow. When you buy rib eyes from your butcher, make sure to ask that he or she leaves the spinalis on!

### FILET MIGNON / TENDERLOIN

The most expensive cut on the steak, the tenderloin has historically been the jewel of the animal. Recent years, however, have seen it slip in fashionability as foodies finally discovered that it lacks flavor compared to other cuts. This is because the tenderloin—a large, cylindrical muscle that runs up and down the spine from the hind leg, tapering as it gets to the front—is a structural muscle and bears no weight. Always cut completely from the bone, it lacks the marbling of the rib eye or New York, and since the muscle does less work, it has less flavor. But,

as its name implies, it's tender and silky, which continues to make it popular. The tenderloin can be cooked whole or sliced into two- to three-inch pieces, which are steaks known as the filet mignon. At the thickest end of the tenderloin, you can cut a plump steak known as the chateaubriand.

### SIRLOIN

On the other side of the spine from the tenderloin is what we call the sirloin steak, though it can have many names. A popular name for this cut is the New York strip, but it's also been called the strip steak, the Delmonico, and the Kansas City. No matter what it's called, it's still cut from the loin primal and is some of the most valuable meat on the animal. While generally not quite as marbled as the rib eye or as tender as the filet, the New York strip may possess, as its fans like to argue, the most flavor.

### T-BONE / PORTERHOUSE

A crosswise cut across the loin of the cow yields a bone in the shape of a T, with meat on each side of the central column. On one side is the tenderloin meat, while on the other you'll have sirloin. This T cut defines both the T-bone and the porterhouse, the difference between them being that the porterhouse (a giant, impressive cut) is taken from farther back on the animal, where the tenderloin is wider. People who love these cuts do so in part because they get to enjoy two cuts in one steak—a piece of the tenderloin for heightened tenderness, and a piece of the sirloin for more flavor. The porterhouse offers more of the tenderloin, while on the T-bone, the tenderloin is but a small morsel.

# NEW SCHOOL CUTS

## FLAT IRON

An absolutely delicious piece of meat, the flat iron is an interesting example of the continuing evolution of butchery. This cut was developed in 2002 by researchers at the Universities of Florida and Nebraska. According to a 2007 release from the University of Florida, "the research to produce leaner and more convenient beef products was initiated when demand for chuck, round, and 'thin cuts'—which make up 73 percent of total beef carcass weight—declined by more than 20 percent from 1980 to 1998." A beef trade group decided that "a more concentrated effort was needed to study the cause for the decreased demand . . . [and] wanted to find out what could be done to reverse the trend and increase the demand for the chuck and round cuts."

Consider the trend reversed, as the result of this investigation is the wonderful flat iron steak, a cut that's become popular at Knife and across the country. The flat iron is a "blade steak" taken from deep in the shoulder of the animal. Because of an inconvenient and impenetrable seam of sinew in the middle of the piece, it had been included with the rest of the chuck and usually ground into hamburger meat. But the researchers found a way to work around and discard the sinew. By cutting the piece in half, lengthwise, you end up with two delicious and easy-to-cook flat irons, a great and economical piece.

Flat Iron

## CULOTTE

This is the cap of the top sirloin butt. In Brazil, it's also known as the *picaña*. Here it might be marketed as top sirloin. It's lean, but I really love the flavor. That leanness also makes it somewhat chewy, so most chefs recommend marination to soften up the cut before cooking.

## TRI-TIP

Introduced as a separate cut in Oakland in the 1950s, the tri-tip has become the signature cut of Central California, thus it's also known as the Santa Maria steak or even the Newport steak. Not far off from the culotte, it comes from the bottom sirloin. A big, chunky piece of meat, it's also flavorful and tough and thus merits marinating and cooking only to medium rare.

Culotte

Tri-Tip

### FLANK STEAK

The flank steak comes from the lower belly, the flank primal. This muscle and the two others near it have the unremitting task of supporting cattle's plentiful abdominal organs, so they can be quite chewy. Yet the flavor's great, and with marination or tenderization, this can be a delicious cut to eat as a thin steak.

### SKIRT

The outside skirt connects to the diaphragm, essential for breathing. Therefore, the skirt muscle gets heavily used, a sign of toughness. However, many tough cuts also have great flavor, and the skirt is a great example of this. With its sinewy, fibrous texture, the skirt can be chewy, but when it's tender enough, it's a delicious steak.

### HANGER STEAK

The hanger steak is another part of the diaphragm, which hangs from the loin, between the kidneys. It has a heavily pronounced grain. The epitome of the "butcher's steak," because of its uniqueness and flavor (sitting so close to the kidneys can give it a deeper, subtly organ-inflected flavor), it's only recently become fashionable. But it's juicy and delicious and wonderful when served medium rare.

# DRY AGING BEEF

What makes a steak great? It should be tender, complex, beefy, but also with earthy, gamy, and sweet notes. It must be juicy, with just the right amount of pushback against the teeth. We're lucky to encounter such steaks every once in a long while. Now imagine all those qualities, but turned up a notch or three. Imagine the flavor of good beef, and then concentrate it exponentially while adding secondary and tertiary flavors of truffles, popcorn, mushrooms, soy, blue cheese—basically the headiest, richest, deepest sensations of narcotized umami possible. That's the attraction of well-aged beef. There's literally nothing like it. That's why we are aging meat to sometimes extreme degrees. We're not simply dry aging for a week or two, as many steakhouses might. Or 21 days. A good average for us is 45 days, but we don't stop there. We also offer 100, 150, and even 240 days—eight months!—when in stock. Lately, we've even experimented with 400-day dry-aged beef. Such extreme spacewalks into the ether of beef umami are not hard to accomplish; they simply require a great deal of discipline, precision, money, and, of course, time.

The aging of meat is nothing new. Indeed, going way back in the history of civilization, meat was often aged, even though ancient peoples had neither the facilities nor technology to do it as precisely as we do now. According to food scientist and author Harold McGee's *On Food and Cooking*, in the 1800s, "beef and mutton joints would be kept at room temperature for days or weeks, until the outside was literally rotten." The French, Bloom notes, called this process *mortification*, and the greatest chef of the day professed that it should be carried on "as far as possible." But that's because when the rotten flesh was cut away, the interior meat was both tenderer and more flavorful. Back then, the animals being consumed were likely already much tougher and more powerfully flavored (they'd be older at slaughter and would have spent a lifetime roaming freely) than the meat we enjoy today.

I remember the first time the potency of dry-aged steak really hit home for me. It was years ago at a cooking conference, where I watched chef David Burke roast a whole beef rib rack that had been dry aged for fifty days. When some of the water is removed, steak can achieve a certain texture—smooth and soft but dense. After roasting, he let it rest, and I noticed that while it rested, not a drop of juice came out. I was fascinated by that unusual detail. Then I tasted it and was absolutely floored by the meat's density, gentle texture, and powerful flavor.

I never forgot that feeling, and when we had the opportunity to open up Knife, I wanted to further investigate the idea of serious dry aging—to bring something new to diners and to further my own personal search for the extremes of deliciousness.

## THE METHOD AND THE MADNESS

The term *dry-aged* gets tossed around a lot, but it's only been in past few years that it's started to really capture the imagination of foodies on a large scale. One place was way out ahead of this curve—Carnevino in Las Vegas. Since they opened it in 2008, Mario Batali and Adam Perry Lang have been taking beef aging to previously unheard of degrees.

I wanted to bring something special to Dallas and to my steakhouse, so I sought out Mario and Adam and asked them if I could come visit to see how it's done. Incredibly graciously, they agreed to teach me, and that's where the beef-aging program at Knife comes from. Now I'm taking it in my own direction, adding things like dry-aged foie gras and pork into the mix of proteins we serve.

Getting a restaurant open is hard enough as it is. But getting it open with an aging locker filled with meat makes it even harder. First of all, it's the investment. Think about it this way: A huge investment for any new restaurant is the wine cellar—both storage and inventory. The nice thing about wine, though, is that it takes care of itself. As long as you keep it at the right temperature and humidity (which can easily be done with a little cheap insulation and a common air conditioner) it not only keeps but it increases in value over years. And if your plans change, you can always sell the wine, usually at a tidy profit.

Beef aging is a different game altogether. The cost of entry is a barrier. First you've got to build a highly precise aging room with perfect temperature, humidity, and airflow control. For us, that was $50,000 right off the bat, not to mention the square footage that you're subtracting from your dining room (which is why most steakhouses age their beef off-site). Then you've got to fill your new refrigerator with tens of thousands of dollars of meat and hope for the best. If something goes awry, you can't sell off the meat at a handsome profit. Rather, it's going into the trash. But we thought this was a risk worth taking.

Part of that was because I'd seen the power of that aged steak. When we announced Knife, we had a little press event. Carnevino had magnanimously sent me home with three of their 240-day aged "risevera" steaks. I cooked one for the staff so they could get an idea of what they'd have the opportunity to cook. The other two I sliced and fed to the press so they could understand what we were trying to do. When I saw their faces light up in amazement, I knew we were going to be okay.

## HOW DRY AGING WORKS

In beef, aging provides the same magic it does for cheese and wine. It increases complexity and umami and smooths texture. Aging meat requires a cold room at a specific humidity with constant airflow. We keep our room at 36 degrees F and 40 percent humidity. The cold and dryness inhibit the growth of microbes and bacteria. In this process, the meat's structure is physically altered by a slow chemical process. Acting on the meat are the very enzymes that animated it when it was live flesh. According to Harold McGee, once the animal's cells are no longer living and able to control them, these enzymes begin to attack the cells, breaking larger compounds into more complex, smaller ones that are full of flavor. At the same time other enzymes—calpains and cathepsins—begin to act on the muscle fibers, slowly eating away at the fibers that make the meat tough and dry. Furthermore, the cathepsins act on the connective tissue, converting more of it into soft, luscious gelatin while at the same time causing the meat to lose less moisture. It's a win-win all around, and the jellification we see on well-aged steaks is one of its more irresistible features.

Over time, there is moisture loss, but it's not so much that it leaves the meat lacking in

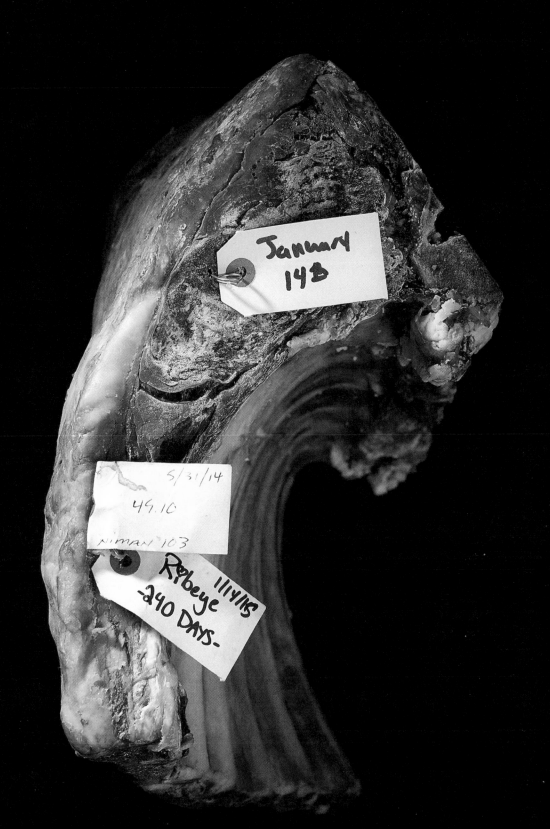

juiciness. This is for a couple of reasons. One, we age the rib eyes as full, uncut racks, up to six to eight bones per large piece. This means that the only exposed meat is on the ends. This meat will become dry and discolored over the weeks and months, but it is trimmed away, leaving the interior, which remains pristine, aged only by enzymes. We also age with the fat cap on these rib racks. The fat protects the interior of the meat from losing too much moisture. Over the course of several weeks, the meat loses a negligible amount of water, but over eight to nine months, we expect the beef to lose around a third of its weight. That's partially what makes it so expensive. But that's also what makes it great. The loss of moisture concentrates the remaining juices and texture, making a more intense bite of steak.

And, yes, it's more expensive, significantly more than our cheapest steak. But the aspect that no one talks about is that the flavor of the meat is so intense, you don't need to eat as much. And when I say that you don't need to eat as much, what I really mean is that you can't and won't eat as much. After a few bites of a 240, you'll find yourself satiated. It's quite remarkable, because it suggests that we don't necessarily feel fullness because of how much we eat but because of how satisfied we are. For those who want to splurge on a 100, 150, or 240, I recommend sharing a couple of different steaks among the table, because the old stuff is really that intense. The 240 is interesting and exotic, but I think the steaks are really at their best in the 150-day range.

## AGED MEAT AT HOME

There are a few good reasons to age steak at home, but also a convincing number of reasons why it might not be worth the trouble. Here are the pros and cons as I see them.

### Pros

First and foremost is price. To buy an aged steak online or from a local butcher (if you're lucky enough to have the rare local butcher that dry ages meat) is expensive. It will likely cost at least $30 a pound for beef aged between thirty and forty-five days, increasing steadily as you get past that. So to buy an aged bone-in rib eye (because it will be aged on the bone) that might weigh 1.5–2 pounds is going to set you back $50–$60. And that's including a fair bit of fat and the bone that you obviously won't eat. So aging at home can cut the cost.

Two, if you're that into steak that you'd be saving significant money, you might enjoy overseeing the aging process. It's not exactly riveting, but you can dial it in yourself to find what degree of aging you most prefer and at what temperature and humidity. It's also an impressive thing to be able to share with guests, much like pulling an old bottle of wine from the cellar.

**Cons**

Logistics. You can't really age meat in your family refrigerator. Opening and closing the door all the time is a no-no, not to mention that all the other foods in the fridge will introduce diverse microbes into the environment. So you'll need a second refrigerator devoted solely to the practice of aging meat. And it has to be big enough to hold a few racks far enough apart that no bit of them touch. You'll also need to equip that fridge with a fan, because air circulation is an important part of the equation. This is a fridge and a fan you'll need to keep going for forty to forty-five days, which is the minimum I believe you need to let meat go for it to start acquiring the salient characteristics of age. Finally, you'll need to figure out some way of controlling the humidity in this refrigerator.

If you, say, convert a mini refrigerator—for instance, the size often used in dorm rooms—for this purpose, you won't be able to age more than a full rack or two, because of space. If you use a full-sized refrigerator, it's going to suck up a lot of energy and space. To make it worthwhile, you'll want to maximize the space by aging as much meat as possible. Will you eat that much when it's ready?

Custom-designed meat-aging units intended for the home consumer are hitting the market these days, and they probably work well, but they can be expensive and space consuming. To give up that kind of cash and space, you have to ask yourself how much long-aged steak you'll really eat and decide if the costs pencil out.

## A Heavenly Pairing

It's not rocket science that red meat and red wine go hand in hand. Indeed, it's a foregone conclusion that pretty much every table in a steakhouse is going to order a red wine. America's love of beef is probably the single greatest reason the Napa Valley is what it is today. We gotta wash down that beef with a juicy, dark Cab. Or do we?

Meat may be the greatest excuse to guzzle Cabernet Sauvignon, but not our super-dry-aged stuff. To go with a 100, 150, or 240, I've found the most magical pairing is not Cabernet. It's not even a red wine. It's white Burgundy—an expensive white wine from France made from Chardonnay. To put it alongside a well-aged steak is a revelation, and you'll never go back.

How can this be, you ask? White wine with red meat? It works on several different levels. First, remember that the aged steak is so intense it can fill you up after just a few bites. That's no joke. It's juicy, rich, and mind-bogglingly dense with flavor. Yes, a red wine's flavor could complement that. But what you really find after taking a bite of this steak is that you want contrast; you want relief from the intensity. White Burgundy is intensely flavored, but it's also bright, lighter, and full of acidity. It refreshes your mouth after the steak, rather than doubling down on heaviness and intensity. Furthermore, the flavors of white Burgundy range from lemon to hazelnuts to fresh cream and butter. As it turns out, they go beautifully with the notes of mushroom, popcorn, and modest blue cheese supplied by the meat. I cannot recommend this enough.

EQUIPMENT

It's easy to geek out on equipment these days. Every time I turn around, there's a new Internet-based kitchen store touting cutting-edge gadgets that will take all guesswork out of cooking, simplify your life, and amaze your friends. Sure, some kitchen gadgets are helpful, and some tools may help you take your cooking to a higher level. Mostly, however, they just offer a false promise of kitchen success through the all-American, pain-free, time-saving tradition of charging your credit card. Shopping may give us a hopeful sense of possibility, but just as the world's most expensive camera won't turn a beginner into Annie Leibovitz or an expensive laptop doesn't guarantee a writer the Pulitzer Prize, the most advanced range of kitchen gear won't turn a home cook into Jacques Pépin.

That said, good tools are essential—it's just that most of the necessary ones were identified centuries ago. This book is about classic cooking techniques, and classic tools are all that's needed to perform them.

The best tools have a few things in common. They are well designed. They are made from good materials. And they are built to last (i.e., they won't crap out on you in a time of need). Those criteria are worth a little extra money, because quality kitchen tools are not like smart-phones—they won't be outdated in two years. Rather, pay the extra money up front and you will be happy for years as long as you clean your tools properly, practice regular maintenance, and hopefully use them regularly. In fact, some tools just get better with age and use, just like a chef.

In this chapter, I'm just going to run down the basics about the tools you might want to have in your kitchen for preparing the recipes in this book with a focus on getting the most out of your steaks and other cuts. Where applicable, I also offer some thoughts on other items that aren't necessary but which come up frequently in conversation with home cooks.

# KNIFE

It's the namesake of my restaurant, so you'd better believe I have some thoughts on this tool. It's also one of the oldest human implements, the ultimate necessity for any carnivore with opposable thumbs. After all, you need a knife to hunt, butcher, cook, and eat meat. We're living in a glorious time for knives thanks to the fact that the American culinary revolution, the yup-pification of the kitchen, and the Internet have breathed new life into the art of knife making. Now with a simple mouse click on your office computer, you can purchase hand-forged knives from both Japanese masters and Brooklyn hip-sters. You have access to knives made of all kinds of materials, from carbon and stainless steel to titanium alloys, ceramics, obsidian, and even plastic. In the steel category alone you can find Japanese steel, Swedish steel, stainless, carbon, Damascus steel, and more. The array of styles

at cooking stores might make you feel like you need to have a collection like a handyman's socket set—long chef's knife, short chef's knife, peeler, paring knife, fish knife, boning knife, cleaver, bread knife, grapefruit knife, cheese knife, and so on. Online, you can find someone to vouch for every different kind. It can get confusing.

Now here's where you might expect me to say that all you need is one knife (and, technically, that's true). I actually think it's good to have a few options, especially if you're going to buy larger cuts of meat and do some butchering at home. But you don't need twenty knives or even ten. Just a few good ones will do. And when I say *good*, I mean knives that are sharp and well made. And you don't need to spend an arm and a leg. A good knife might cost a bit more up front, but don't jeopardize your retirement fund. A lot of it depends on how you plan to use it. If you value good tools and are likely

to take care of them, you might buy something more high end. If you don't particularly plan on nurturing your knives, get a cheap, plastic-handled version from a restaurant supply store for twenty dollars and you're good to go.

The one knife you'll surely need is a basic chef's knife. This a classic wedge-shaped knife that can be used for anything—slicing, chopping, crushing, mincing. The classic French chef's knife is what I grew up using and still use. Today, people usually think about them in two styles—European and Japanese. The main difference is that Japanese knives are considered a little bit thinner and more delicate and are made from a brittler kind of steel because they are sharpened to an acuter edge, often on only one side of the blade to achieve finer slicing, which is a hallmark of Japanese cooking. The French-style knives I grew up using, on the other hand, are perhaps not as sharp, but are heavier, more durable, and perhaps more versatile.

When it comes to steel, the major categories are stainless and carbon steel. The difference here is obvious to the eye. Stainless steels are alloys designed not to rust. Consequently, they are a little harder, meaning that in general they don't take quite as fine an edge as carbon steel, but may hold the edge for a little longer. Carbon steel, on the other hand, gets sharper, but loses its edge faster, requiring more frequent sharpening. It also rusts and, therefore, needs to be cleaned and dried immediately after each use. Acid—citrus, especially—will quickly discolor the blade. Carbon steel looks clean coming out of the box, but no matter how meticulous you are in caring for it, it will become discolored. It's not a big deal, just a matter of visual preference. If you want a good knife that's going to last you a long time, clean up easily, and not require a ton of maintenance, just go with a stainless steel ten-inch French-style chef's knife from a major company like Sabatier. That will set you back around eighty dollars. If you want to get fancier, there are plenty of options. And, like I said earlier, if you don't care too much, there are cheaper, even disposable options.

The other cutting implements you might want to have around are simple. A paring knife is good for doing smaller work—peeling, coring, and the like. If you're planning on doing some home butchering, a boning knife, which is usually around six inches long, is very narrow, and has a sharp point, is useful, though not essential. Its maneuverability in tight spaces in between joints and tendons comes in handy. In the same arena of butchering or breaking down a large cut, but with a vastly different purpose, you may want to own a Chinese-style cleaver or some other heavy, somewhat blunt knife that can hack through lighter bones (for heavier ones you'll want a bone saw, but that's starting to get into advanced butchery).

## The Luckiest Day of My Life

I bought this beautiful, razor-sharp Misono eight-inch chef's knife when I started work at RM Seafood. It would be the talisman of the new phase of my life. An inspector from the health board would come and check the kitchen often because we had raw seafood. I got to know her by name, so it was no big deal. But one day she came in, and I was distracted because I was at the same time trying to get the lid off a frozen container of stock . . . and using the knife to do it. Since I wasn't particularly focusing on what I was doing, you guessed it: the knife slid off the top of the icy container and through my hand. It was a straight, almost surgical cut, and the knife was so sharp that it embedded deep in the meat of my palm. I stifled a cry of "Oh sh—!" pulled the knife out, and clamped my other hand over the gash. I was lucky that Chris Janz, the sommelier, happened to be right there. He was a former U.S. Army Ranger and took control of the situation, right under the health inspector's nose. He walked me over to a corner and ran off, coming back quickly with a towel and a bottle of rubbing alcohol. "Bite down," he said, putting the towel between my teeth. "This is going to hurt." Then he emptied the bottle into the wound, eliciting a flash of blinding pain. Then he put gauze on it and wrapped the whole thing up in duct tape, which I would change twice a day for the next two weeks until it had started to heal. It was only because it was so sharp and so precise a cut that I never needed stitches. The knife missed bones, tendons, and anything else of vital importance. For that, it was the luckiest day of my life, and I still have a three-inch scar on my hand to remember it by. (I still have the knife too.)

# SPOON

Before I had Knife, I had Spoon, a restaurant devoted to fish. It's appropriate then that the one personal cooking effect I always travel with—no, I don't bother bringing my own knives on every trip—is a spoon. It comes in handy for many cooking tasks—from portioning spices and stirring sauces to skimming stocks, pan basting meats, and tasting dishes.

For me, there is one true chef's spoon. It's the Gray Kunz sauce spoon, and it's become a cult tool for chefs. Gray was the founding chef of Lespinasse, one of New York's groundbreaking fine-dining restaurants of the 1990s and a place where a number of renowned chefs of today learned their crafts. Starting in 1992, each new chef would be issued a special spoon. It had been designed by Kunz. The back of each spoon was stamped with a unique serial number and the station where the recipient worked. The numbers were recorded in a ledger, ensuring that found spoons could be returned to their owners along with heaping spoonfuls of humiliation for their carelessness. The spoons became such cult objects that Kunz began selling them to the public.

In a 2015 timeline of Lespinasse, *Lucky Peach* magazine had the following to say about the spoon: "Measuring exactly nine inches, it is a bridge between a larger cooking spoon and a small saucing spoon. It's big enough to handle robust cooking tasks like basting, roasting, flipping meats, and stirring, but is still small enough and tapered at the tip, so it can be used for more delicate and precise tasks like saucing, making quenelles, and portioning." It's also deeper than most spoons—its bowl holds exactly 2.5 tablespoons. The sole vendor, JB Prince, still sells them for around twelve dollars each. You won't regret owning one.

# CASSETTE BURNER

Now, those of you who live in houses or have luxurious home kitchens may think of the humble cassette burner as an optional piece of equipment. But hear me out: You want one of these. The cassette burner is an essential piece in my Back to the Pan method for cooking steaks.

Cooking steaks in a pan indoors generates billowing smoke and spews a fine cloud of fat and grease into the air. You'll notice this not only when you wipe down the stove top afterward but also on all the surrounding walls. If your kitchen has shelves instead of cabinets, you'll find that sticky, fine coating of grease on every dish and glass standing on those shelves. Unless you clean those too every day, they'll attract dust, which will stick to the grease.

A cassette burner is simply a portable gas burner, just like the one you have on your gas stove. It's the same concept as the portable camping stoves, but much better. I use them when I do off-site gigs, and they work fantastically well, even for a chef used to cooking over the blasting blue flames of a restaurant range. Most cassette burners are fueled by butane cartridges that are inexpensive, easy to procure, and even easier to use.

The burner itself is light and takes up little space. Apartment dwellers, you can take it out on your balcony. New York City residents might find themselves considering their fire escapes (though that's technically illegal). The point is that you can sizzle steaks without smoking your place out and covering your kitchen with grease. If you have a porch or a backyard, set it up out there. Cleanup is a cinch; no more than ten seconds are needed to set up and break down.

As for power, a good cassette burner is comparable to or better than the conventional range most people have in their apartments or homes. The average burner on that home range clocks in at around 7,000 BTUs. In contrast, it's not hard to find cassette burners for under forty dollars that heat up to 8,000 or 12,000 BTUs, and for a little more money up to 15,000 BTUs. By the way, 12,000 is plenty of heat to get a good sear on a steak or nice browning on a burger. There are a few brands out there, but the major player is a Japanese company called Iwatani.

I'm not the first chef to tout these products in print. None other than the late, great Pierre Franey—former chef of New York's Le Pavillon, television cooking star, and writer of *The New York Times*' "60-Minute Gourmet" column in the 1970s and '80s—mentioned the Iwatani in a *Times* piece way back in 1983.

*For years I have been on the lookout for a portable gas heating unit with enough power to match a kitchen range, but the closest things I could find were Sterno units or other alcohol-powered devices that are designed for warming, not for cooking. They just don't have the output to sear a steak or reduce a sauce. Now I have come across a remarkable new portable burner called the Cassette Feu (model A-7), made by a Japanese company, Iwatani. This powerful, cleverly designed device virtually simulates range-top cooking; it may keep me out of the kitchen much of this summer.*

I couldn't have said it better myself.

# MEAT GRINDER

Any serious carnivore these days should have the ability to grind meat at home. It's not only a question of taste and deliciousness but a question of food security. You can read more about this in chapter 6, Burgers and Other Sandwiches, but the safest ground meat is the stuff you grind yourself. The second safest is what you ask your local butcher to grind for you at the time of order. And the third safest is probably what your local butcher grinds in advance and offers from his or her display case. And when I use the term *local butcher*, I don't mean the guys behind the counter, who weigh and wrap the meat at your local supermarket. I mean a local butcher whose name you know. If you aren't so lucky to have one of those, you'll want that meat grinder.

We use the meat grinder every day. We grind beef tartare to order, we make incredible meatballs, and sometimes we'll grind our burger meat (though we go through so much of it that our tendency is to get it straight from 44 Farms, who grinds it to our specifications; there's no more direct and safer source than buying the meat directly from those who raise it).

Don't be afraid of the meat grinder. It's the simplest of devices, easy to use, and generally easy to clean up (as long as you have a good one). The main factor in selecting one should be the amount of power it has. Grinding is tough on a motor, so you need something both powerful and durable. Nothing is worse than having your grinder jam on you when you have pounds of meat left to run. So choose well.

The simplest solution for a serious home cook is the KitchenAid stand mixer, because you may already own one. KitchenAid makes a meat-grinding attachment that makes use of the mixer's motor by simply screwing onto the front end of the machine. It's pretty well powered and works impressively. The only downside I can see is that it offers only two choices of plate sizes, coarse and less coarse. A fine setting might be nice, but those two are sufficient for what you'll do in this book and most stuff beyond. Plus, KitchenAid sells this for around fifty dollars. Beyond this, there are some stand-alone units made by the likes of Waring that get high marks, but they are much more expensive than the stand mixer (which also, of course, kneads dough, mixes cakes, fluffs egg whites, extrudes pasta, and more). At the restaurant, our meat grinder is just a giant, industrial version of the KitchenAid stand mixer.

# CARBON STEEL PANS

In the aisles of high-end cooking stores, the gleaming silver disks of All-Clad and burnished copper shimmer of Mauviel beckon like gems at a jewelry store. These are lovely and effective cookware brands. But if you want to cook like a chef and especially if you want to effortlessly sear steaks, brown chops, and crisp perfect burgers, you'll want to use what I've been using my entire career—carbon steel pans. And I'm far from the only chef who uses these. In fact, most chefs I know use carbon steel, definitely in European kitchens and in many great American ones.

Depending on the treatment they receive or the brand, you might also hear these pans referred to as blue steel, black steel, and more. The exact brand we use in all my restaurants is called Blackline SwissSteel, and we get it through a company called Spring USA (which used to only sell through wholesale channels to restaurants, but recently, I've seen their pans crop up on retail sites).

Here are the major differences among carbon steel, cast iron, and stainless steel pans. Stainless steel is an alloy of iron and chromium and sometimes nickel. Carbon steel and cast iron are actually much more alike, with carbon steel (despite the name) containing less carbon than cast iron. For what it's worth, stainless is lighter and prettier than both, but doesn't conduct heat as well, is less durable, and doesn't develop a functionally nonstick surface; indeed, food often sticks to it. However, it is nice and shiny and won't rust or corrode. Stainless steel is also impervious to the acidity in certain foods (tomatoes, vinegar), while carbon steel and cast iron are not. Cost-wise, there's a big difference. Stainless steel pans tend to run almost twice as much as comparable carbon steel, which in turn is more expensive than cast iron.

Cast iron and carbon steel behave rather similarly, but because of its higher iron content, the carbon steel is less brittle than cast iron. While this doesn't functionally make a difference to most people, it means, in theory, that carbon steel can be formed into a lighter pan than a cast iron pan of the same size without sacrificing performance (my Spring USA pans are quite hefty, though, only marginally lighter than cast iron—but unless you're sautéing with these big boys, it doesn't really matter).

What I really love about carbon steel is that it's a little nimbler and more responsive than cast iron. On the stove, it heats up quickly and distributes the heat evenly around the pan. Yet it also reacts rapidly to changes in temperature. If you need to turn down the heat, for instance, the pan cools quickly.

Both cast iron and carbon steel pans require seasoning, while stainless steel doesn't. This means treating the surface of the pan with heat and oil (or some other kind of fat) repeatedly before first use. If you prize convenience, this process can be a little bit of a pain and does take some time, but I think it's worth it. That's because with proper seasoning, your carbon steel pan will become effectively nonstick. By coating the pan with oil in the presence of high heat, you cause the oil to bond to the metal. The resulting surface is unreal—naturally nonstick and free of Teflon or any other laboratory-engineered coating that can leach into your food or easily scratch. With a well-seasoned carbon steel plan, you can fry eggs, make omelets, cook fish without any mess. And the advantage over conventional nonstick pans is that you can use any sort of metal implement like tongs or a spatula without damaging the surface. It's really the perfect pan.

To season, first you scrub off the shipping grease and any bit of metal filings left over from the manufacturing process. Do this with hot water and a sponge. Then follow the instructions that come with the pan for proper seasoning or research your own desired method. Some people recommend cooking the peels of potatoes in heaps of salt and oil in the pan. For some, it involves heating the pan with salt. For most people, though, seasoning simply requires heating the pan in a 500-degree F oven for an hour or so after rubbing a few drops of high-temperature resistant oil into it. Repeat this process a few times and you'll be good to go.

If there's a drawback to carbon steel and cast iron, it's that they're reactive to acids and can rust if not cared for properly. But proper care is quick and painless. It will prevent the pan from rusting and greatly diminish the reaction with acidic foods. Nevertheless, I wouldn't use the carbon steel pan to cook tomatoes or simmer tomato sauce (it's highly acidic), and we don't use them to make pan sauces for the steaks (that is, deglaze with vinegar or wine and then reduce to make a sauce for the meat in the same pan that you used to sear the meat).

Care and maintenance is easy. Just continue to cook with the pans—the layers of seasoning will just continue to improve over time. After use, wash the pans out with hot water and a gentle scrubbing—no soap—and then dry them slowly over a low flame on the stove top and rub in a few drops of vegetable oil. Buy a couple of these pans, season them, and care for them well, and you'll enjoy a lifetime of great cooking.

# THER—MOMETER

A quick search on the Internet will deliver all kinds of methods for testing the doneness of a steak—my favorite is the one about matching the softness of the steak to the fleshy firmness of parts of your hand. But there's a better solution—why not just find out the exact temperature by reading it directly? A quick-reading thermometer is a good investment. Puncturing a steak once or twice to glean the internal temperature isn't going to cause it to leak all its juices, and the information you gain about when to take it off and how long to rest it can be the difference between a ruined meal and an unforgettable one.

STEAK

There's nothing better than a perfectly cooked steak. And there's nothing worse than a poorly cooked one. In theory, nothing's simpler than cooking a steak; it's a layup. On the other hand, cooking steak perfectly, every time? Not so easy. Few things carry the pressure—steak's one of the most expensive meats, and there's no fixing an overcooked one.

Even the pros miss layups. While working on this book, I was in New Orleans for a night and found myself at a steakhouse, where I was treated to one of the worst steaks I've ever had. Aged for thirty days, it cost well over fifty dollars. I understand that it was New Orleans, which is touristy, but this was inexcusable. It wasn't a bad piece of meat; it just wasn't cooked properly. Actually, that's being nice—it was defiled! The outside was gray and striped with cheesy, dark grill marks. The inside was tough and flavorless. For this, there can be no excuse.

People think you have to go to a steakhouse to get the highest quality experience, but, as my experience in New Orleans shows, that's no guarantee. Steakhouses used to have access to the best meat. But in the age of the Internet, when high-quality beef is just a click away, none of this stands any longer. The goal of this chapter—of this book—is to show you how to make classic steakhouse-quality steak at home.

The only thing most people don't have at home is a steak broiler that sizzles the meat at 800 degrees. In a restaurant where, during the busy times in an evening, we're putting out dozens of steaks an hour, the steak broiler is the best way to get a deep sear on a piece of meat without overcooking the inside—and doing it really fast.

But at home, the ability to do multiple steaks at once isn't much of an issue—and you don't need a broiler. So what are the advantages of cooking steak *chez vous*? One, obviously, is that it's better. You can get meat of supreme quality from trustworthy sources nowadays and cook it as you wish with convenience and minimal effort. Two is control. Many steakhouses bathe their meat in butter, add flavorings, and have dull side dishes. At home, you can craft the meal as you want. You can keep steak healthier with a drizzle of olive oil or nothing at all. The final advantage is price. What you can simply make at home can equal the quality of many a steakhouse at just a fraction of the price, especially when you throw in the cost of sides, tip, and wine.

But most important is cooking it to juicy, crusty, meaty perfection, and the surest way I know how to do this is the method I call Back to the Pan. Cooking a steak in a skillet is, in some ways, old fashioned. But guys like me, who've been around the block a few times, are here to remind you that sometimes the older generations knew what they were doing. Back to the Pan is a classic method that I update with some tweaks that will result in the best possible steak you can make at home. And you don't have to take the time to build a coal bed or get your hands dirty in a bag of charcoal. It's quick, simple, and the key to the best steak you've ever put in your mouth.

# BACK TO
# THE PAN

Somehow over the years, ownership of the imagery of steak was claimed by the grill. Live-fire cookery is fashionable these days. But in the case of steak, when someone wants to get your mouth watering, whether in a food magazine spread or a television commercial for Outback Steakhouse, the image inevitably is of wisps of orange fire crackling under a glistening steak branded heavily with grill marks.

Not that there's anything wrong with that, but using live fire to cook your rib eye is the easiest way to ruin the meat. While a little smoky char from wood coals can be nice, we've all seen how hard fire can be to manage: The steaks get overcooked or, even worse, burned because the fire's too hot or dripping fat causes flare-ups that scorch the steak.

The solution to this problem is simple, elegant, and convenient: I give you the heavy steel pan. Compared to the open flame, with proper cooking technique in a pan, you can get a superior crust, never have to worry about burning, and not have to take the time or effort to fire up the coals or get the gas grill hot. A good pan can make a cheaper cut taste better, and it intensifies the savor of great beef.

With regard to cooking with fire, I don't mind the flavor of a little smoke now and then. But if I have a really great piece of meat—which I always do—I want to taste the beef as intimately and intensely as possible. The pan amplifies this by a factor of degrees.

## THE CRUST OF THE MATTER

People worry most about the interior doneness of a steak. And while cooking a steak to desired temperature is important, just as crucial to great-tasting steak is the exterior—the crust. Think about it. The crust is where the salt infiltrates the meat, creating synergies of salty beefiness. It's the toasted, crunchy contrast to the tender meat inside. And it's where the real flavor complexity resides thanks to the Maillard reactions that cause the browning. The diagonal or crosshatched grill marks advertisers like to use to make their steaks look succulent? They are tasty. But if the grill marks are the most delicious part of the meat, why have just a few of them? Why shouldn't the entire surface of the meat be browned? It should.

People call the browning of meat "caramelization," but that's not the whole story. Caramelization is what happens with sugar. When you have substances that are not foremost composed of sugar—such as the protein in meat—the reactions that cause the browning are known as the Maillard reactions, after the French scientist who studied them around 1910. Thanks to the presence of substances like amino acids with the naturally occurring sugars, Maillard reactions produce complex, meaty flavors. The reactions start to occur in the relatively low temperature range between 250 and 330 degrees F and speed up with higher heat. Getting a good crust on your meat doesn't depend on ridiculous amounts of heat, but higher temperatures speed up the evaporation of water and accelerate the browning reactions.

## RENDERING

As you cook a steak in a pan, one thing that's preserved is the meat's fat, which quickly melts or renders due to the heat. Over charcoal, the rendered fat drips out of the meat into the fire and either flames up and can burn the meat or is otherwise lost. The great side benefit of cooking the steak in a pan is that the fat is preserved in the pan and becomes part of the cooking medium. You end up cooking the meat in its own fat, doubling down on the beefy goodness, while preserving the meat's juices. Of course, you don't consume this fat—it is left behind in the pan when the steak is finished—but it becomes a powerful agent in building flavor.

## PRECISION CONTROL WITH *POÊLÉ*

There are few things more annoying than a bald, underdone splotch on the otherwise wonderfully dark, roasted crust of a steak. One of the challenges of fully browning a piece of meat, whether on the grill, in a pan, or in the oven, is to get that spot brown. The various solutions usually involve pressing down on the meat or laying something heavy on it to get that area of the surface in contact with the heat source. Chefs trained with classical technique have another method. It's not hard to master and is a beautiful way to finish a steak. The French word for it is *poêlé* (pronounced pwuh-LAY), which simply means to cook in a frying pan. But the word has evolved to refer to pan basting.

The technique is easy and only requires a spoon. After a few minutes, the meat will be sizzling in a shallow pool of its own fat. Or at this point, a French chef will classically add a hunk of butter and some aromatic seasonings like a few sprigs of thyme and a clove of garlic. The action is simply to tilt the pan enough for the hot fat to pool in the bottom of the pan and to spoon it over the meat. It crackles for a second and then runs back down into the bottom of the pan. Repeat this rapidly over and over to finish cooking while sizzling the uneven surfaces of the meat in the flavorful butter or fat. It's a great way to attack those pesky spots that haven't browned on their own.

# HOW TO COOK PERFECT STEAK, BACK TO THE PAN

**1. Choose your meat** ★ For the full-length discussion of meat, look to chapter 2, Beef. Any cut that can be cooked on a grill or in a broiler can be cooked Back to the Pan. Here I'll just say, when you find a good source of steak, stick with it. If you've got that awesome butcher, shop there and happily spend a little extra for good beef. It's worth the dollars to eat less but better beef. You can also order meat online from top-quality ranches and butchers. They'll send it frozen, which is not a problem. So long as you thaw it well, there's nothing wrong with a frozen steak—meat quality does not suffer from this.

**2. Select what cut you want** ★ The various cuts are also described in chapter 2, Beef, but it's important to consider what piece you're cooking before you put it on. Rib eyes, New Yorks, and filet mignons are all more marbled and tender. They're also more expensive. New School or butcher's cuts like flat irons, hangers, or skirts have less marbling and will be cheaper. They're all delicious. If you select 100 percent grass-fed beef, know that it quite likely will be a little tougher than beef that has been finished on grain. If that's the case, you may want to cook it a little rarer to get the best texture.

**3. Gauge the size of the steak and get a feel for it** ★ Here's where you really examine the meat before you get ready to cook it. Thickness is a major factor. The thicker the steak, the longer it will take to cook the interior. The thinner the steak, the hotter the pan needs to be, because you need to develop the crust quickly before the interior gets overcooked. If you like rare and medium-rare steaks, you may generally prefer thicker cuts one to four inches in width. Touch the steak and feel its density. Feeling it when it's raw will help give an indication of how done it's getting during cooking.

**4. Pull the steak from the refrigerator** ★ The idea of letting the steak warm up to room temperature is good on paper, but to actually warm to room temperature takes a lot longer than the half hour most cookbooks recommend, and it's also not exactly the safest way to handle meat. Frozen meat should be thoroughly defrosted, but if it's still cold, that's not a problem. Never defrost in a microwave. The most even and rapid way is to put a vacuum-sealed steak in a bowl of room-temperature water for thirty to forty-five minutes, which should be ample time to bring it out of a frosty state. Make sure the meat is pliant and soft before cooking it. But don't worry about it being room temperature when you cook it. Steak heats up so quickly in the pan that letting the steak's surface come to room temp (while the interior remains frigid, anyway) is unnecessary. Not to mention that you might want thinner cuts of steak to be downright cold when you

cook them, as you'll be able to cook the exterior longer to develop that crust while the cold interior heats more slowly. Really thick cuts will probably have to finish cooking in the oven, so it really doesn't matter much if they're cool.

### 5. Dry the steak completely ★ One of
the most important factors in creating a good crust is starting with dry meat. That's because it steals energy from the hot pan to evaporate residual moisture on the steak, cooling the pan. Furthermore, surface moisture creates steam, and steaming meat inhibits the formation of the all-important crust. So either dry steaks by hand with paper towels or let them sit for a few hours uncovered in the fridge until the surface doesn't glisten with moisture.

### 6. Heat the pan and preheat the oven (if needed) ★ If you're cooking it outside the
house on a cassette burner, set that up on a stable surface where you have a little room to move around. Otherwise, put your carbon steel or cast-iron pan over high heat. Give it a few minutes to heat up. I think all the talk about heating a cast-iron pan in a 500-degree-F oven for thirty minutes is overkill. Part of the pan process is to make things easier and more efficient. Turning your house into an oven for the sole purpose of heating a pan goes too far. The pan can get plenty hot in just three to four minutes.

### 7. Generously coat the meat on all sides with salt and black pepper ★ There are
many approaches to salting steak. Some people salt it a day or two in advance so that some of the salt seeps in a little deeper than the outer coat of the meat. And some like to salt it just before cooking. Either one works well, so long as the salt is applied far enough in advance or just before cooking. Salt pulls water out of meat. If you add salt more than a minute or two before cooking, you're going to be trying to sear meat that's leaking water, making it very difficult to create a crust. Salting in advance should therefore be done a couple of hours and up to a day before cooking so the surface of the meat can dry. Or immediately before cooking. The amount of salt is up to you, but I like to give a generous dusting of kosher salt on each side (up to a teaspoon per side, enough to create a nice even white cover). Don't oversalt, as there's no going back. But a dense piece of good beef can handle a good bit of salt.

### 8. Add fat ★ At Knife, we pan cook steaks in
just a little neutral oil. That can be canola, peanut, grapeseed, whatever you want. Don't start with butter or olive oil, however, as their low smoke points will burn the fat before the steak is cooked, causing char and bitterness. Just a quick drizzle of oil is all you need to get the steak going. The oil is not for flavor; rather, it's a conductor of heat to begin the transfer of energy from the pan to the meat. In seconds, the steak will start to render its own fat, adding to what's in the pan.

### 9. Throw on the steak ★ To make sure the
underside of the steak gets coated with oil, immediately after you place it in the hot pan, pick up the steak with your tongs and let the puddle of oil run under it before placing it back in the pan. Allow the steak to sizzle and brown for a few minutes. It's fine to lift an edge of the meat to gauge progress.

### 10. Flip the steak and adjust the heat ★
When the first side has developed a nice crust— the meat has turned a rich shade of reddish

brown and shows visible dryness—flip the steak. Particularly with thicker cuts, it's often necessary to turn down the heat after or even before the flip. This is because the pan has had a chance to recover a lot of the energy it lost to the meat when you put the steak in. The idea that you can only flip a steak once is wrong, although I recommend trying not to flip more than a few times, mainly because you lose track of it and forget which side has cooked more than the other.

You want it to brown steadily and evenly at this point, and super-high heat will result not in a great crust, but in burned meat. To get that perfect browning and more intense seasoning, here's where you might want to *poêlé* and/or add some butter, herbs, or garlic. Likewise, feel free to flip the steak back and forth a couple of times.

**11. Gauge the doneness** ★ You should have a good idea how you like your steak cooked. French people love super-rare meat (they order it *bleu* for barely cooked, raw meat on the inside; *saignant*, meaning bloody, for slightly cooked, but still rare; and *à point* for rare or just barely past rare). Medium rare is how most steak connoisseurs these days seem to order their meat, as anything beyond gets tough and dry. For grass-fed and the less luxurious cuts, a little more on the rare side works well, as they're tougher to begin with. For well-marbled meat, medium rare is nice, as it renders some of the fat on the interior but preserves all the juiciness. Truly rare or raw meat has a pleasing texture, but not much flavor. It's really not until meat is barely cooked that it develops its meaty savor. A thick-cut, bone-in piece like a porterhouse or a

bone-in rib eye will probably need to finish in the oven, as the meat next to the bone will cook more slowly than the rest of the steak. To finish, place the steak in a preheated 400-degree-F oven for a few minutes until the meat next to the bone registers the desired doneness.

Achieving perfect doneness every time takes experience, so getting to know your meat both before and after cooking is important. A rare steak will still be quite tender to the touch. Medium rare will be tender, but with a little bit of firmness. And if the steak is hard and unyielding, it's going to be medium or well done, conditions from which there is no turning back. It's always better to undercook a steak than to overcook it, as you can always put it in the oven or back in the pan to get a few more degrees of finish.

You can also use the most precise form of measuring temperature available—a good meat thermometer. For anyone who loves cooking, investing in an instant-read thermometer is a good idea. For steaks, they're fantastic. Rare meat with a deep red color will be around 120–125 degrees F, medium rare from 125–130 degrees F, and medium at about 135 degrees F. (The USDA, with its unstinting approach to food safety, doesn't recommend serving meat at lower than a 145-degree F internal temperature after a three-minute rest. But I and pretty much every other chef prefer our meat rare to medium rare.)

### 12. Rest the steak, but not too much ★

The old wisdom that steak needs to rest—the longer the better—doesn't really fly anymore. Resting allows for carryover cooking, where the heat from the exterior travels to the interior of the meat, continuing to cook it. Large cuts of meat like roasts can benefit from some resting. But thin steaks don't need to sit more than a minute or two. If the steaks are thicker than a couple of inches, rest them for a few minutes to allow the interior heat to even out. People also discuss resting as allowing for meat to reabsorb juiciness that would otherwise be lost on the plate. If this is true, it's been shown to be only worth a small percentage of the meat's juiciness to begin with, and, anyway, juice that seeps onto the plate is usually mopped up with each bite of meat, meaning that it isn't lost either way. No more than five minutes is needed to rest any steak, which is pretty much the time it takes to get from kitchen to table. An argument against resting is that it's nice to eat steak while it's still warm, not when the exterior has cooled to room temperature.

### 13. Serve the steak ★

With large steaks for two, it can be nice to cut into slices in advance. Particularly if the cut is on the bone, at Knife, we first slice it completely off the bone, then into individual slices. We serve it with the meat back in place next to the bone on a warm plate. For whole individual steaks, I like to serve them uncut as whole slabs, letting the diner do the cutting herself. As always, slice the meat against the grain. If you cut it with the grain, it's going to be terribly tough and chewy. Going against the grain shortens the muscle fibers and makes for wonderfully tender steaks. To do this, first look at the cooked meat and you'll notice that the muscle fibers are all aligned in a certain direction (it's easier to read in tougher cuts like flank or skirt steak than in rib eyes). Then, simply cut across the grain—perpendicular or at some angle that intersects the grain—never parallel.

# OTHER STEAK COOKING METHODS

I may love the classic technique of Back to the Pan, but I also believe there's more than one right way to cook a steak. In fact, at Knife we employ a number of methods: steak broiler, carbon steel pan, sous vide, and wood grill. Here's a rundown on other methods.

## STEAK BROILER

As described earlier, this is a restaurant piece of equipment that few people have at home. It cooks blazing hot, somewhere around 800–900 degrees F. This allows us to get a great sear on the most expensive cuts without overcooking the insides. It also cooks faster than any other method, which is necessary for a high-volume restaurant like Knife.

## SOUS VIDE

This is the "modernist" method that cooks the meat in a plastic bag in water held at a certain temperature. You need a water circulator to keep the temperature consistent. These circulating water baths used to be the domain of restaurants, as they were big, expensive pieces of equipment. But now these are made for the home too, and you can find a circulator for the home for under $200. What these do is cook the meat all the way through to a precise temperature so you never overcook the meat. You like a medium-rare steak at 130 degrees F? Then just set the water to 130 degrees F and cook it in a bag for anywhere from twenty minutes to an hour, depending on the size of piece. Once it reaches the max temperature, it can't overcook. We use this method for our New School cuts like flat irons, as they can be done in advance, held at proper temperature for as long as needed, and then finished on the wood-fired grill.

Sous vide is being advocated more and more for home chefs because it's so foolproof. Cook the inside to the right temperature, then finish it over the grill or in a pan and get the crust afterward. It works just fine, but I still prefer the old method of cooking the steaks. For one, it's easier. You don't have to go through the time to set up and use a water bath. It's more efficient—you don't use a plastic bag that you're just going to throw away. And finally, it connects you to the food—there's a challenge in cooking a steak correctly, and learning how to do it properly is satisfying for any chef. Sous vide may take some of the risk out, but I say, "Nothing ventured, nothing gained."

## WOOD GRILL

At Knife, we have a wood-fired grill in which we burn red oak logs. We use it to finish the New School cuts, which have been precooked sous vide because they tend to take longer to cook than the richer cuts. We like a little kiss of smoke on cuts like the hanger steak and the flat iron—but just a little.

The biggest challenge with cooking steak and developing a crust on a grill is not burning it. It's okay to move the meat, if you're getting flare-ups. But the best thing to avoid burning and flames is to not cook over an active fire. Therefore, the most important part of cooking

on a grill is the coal bed. You don't want to cook over an active flame. It has to be a bed of coals. If you're going to be cooking a lot of steaks over a period of time, you need an extra grill or a firebox to always have fresh coals at the ready, because the others will be constantly burning out.

When I set up the grill for cooking, I create three distinct areas of heat: a searing spot directly over the coals, a finishing spot of lower heat right near the coals, and a holding spot, which is much cooler but still on the grill.

## BIG GREEN EGG

Big Green Eggs are nice tools, but I'm not a fan of them when it comes to grilling steaks. Their best function is as big wood- or charcoal-fired outdoor ovens—great at reaching and holding high temperatures with utmost efficiency. But those high temperatures and efficiency mean that it's hard to grill because it gets so hot—it's like cooking on a stove and in an oven at the same time. Even setting them up for indirect cooking can be difficult, because the smaller ones lack the space to create truly separate temperature ranges. Big Green Eggs (and other Kamado-style cookers) are great, but I like a good old-fashioned grill or hibachi when it comes to steak.

# STEAK CONDIMENTS
## TESAR'S FIVE ESSENTIAL SAUCES FOR STEAK

One summer of my youth when I was working at Club Pierre, Pierre brought in a chef he knew from France. His name was Willie. I don't even remember his last name, but this guy ended up having a profound effect on my life. For that one summer, he came in and cooked with me every day. And I can tell you, this man was a genius of sauces—he taught me everything I know about sauces today. Willie was mysterious and had stories, problems, and baggage—he'd been homeless in Paris and living in a park before Pierre brought him in; he was a drug user and borderline psychotic. But, man, could he make sauces. (He could also open a bottle of wine with a loaf of bread.) I have no idea what became of poor Willie. But his art lives on with me.

Most of the time, a fine steak needs nothing but salt and pepper. But sometimes it's nice to have a little complementary flavor to spice things up. For me, there are five great sauces that complement steak, coming from a few different cultures that all revere the cow. As you'd expect, the French sauces are much more labor and time intensive than the others, but they are versatile and have applications even beyond steak. ★

# BORDELAISE SAUCE

When I first started experiencing French food, I would dine around at the many great French bistros of New York, such as Raoul's. And it was there that I noticed the silky, glistening, flavorful, beefy element in so many of the dishes. It coated meat; it glossed sauces; it even could beef up a fish dish. I was amazed and had to know what this magical elixir was.

Turns out that this classic "brown sauce" is a foundational sauce of France and a fixture in meat cookery, as I learned from Chef Pierre. It's a lush, refined, elegant invocation of beef with a velvety texture and a touch of sweetness. It's called bordelaise, because it comes from the Bordeaux region of France and features red wine as well as shallots, thyme, bay leaf, and veal stock. A few dabs of this sauce on the plate beneath a steak simply doubles down on the beefiness.

Bordelaise and its building block of veal stock rely on a lot of simmering and reducing. You can purchase decent beef or veal stock at most good gourmet grocers nowadays. But if you have the time and inclination, I recommend making your own by long-simmering roasted beef shanks and knuckles with caramelized carrots and onions. Both sauce and stock freeze well and can be retrieved and thawed out for special occasions and to make any simple pan sauce or au poivre sauce. For the red wine, I go by the old adage: "If I can't drink it, I won't cook with it." I also like to add a couple of cups of ruby port wine for depth, balance, and a hint of sweetness.

Before serving, it's nice to finish off the bordelaise by melting in a tablespoon of butter, a dash of black pepper, and even a squeeze of lemon juice to perk it up.

YIELD: 3 CUPS

**5 large shallots, ends trimmed, coarsely chopped**

**3 cups dry red wine, like Cabernet Sauvignon**

**2 cups ruby port**

**3 sprigs fresh thyme**

**2 bay leaves, fresh or dried**

**10 cups (2½ quarts) homemade veal stock or low-sodium beef stock**

In a large saucepan, place the shallots, red wine, port, thyme, and bay leaves. Turn the heat to medium-high and cook, uncovered, until the liquid is almost completely gone (what French chefs call *au sec*), 20–30 minutes. There should be just enough sticky liquid to coat the bottom of the pan.

Add the veal or beef stock and bring the mixture to a simmer. Cook, uncovered, for 1½–2 hours, or until the mixture has reduced by two-thirds; you should have 3–3⅓ cups. The sauce should have a velvety texture and coat the back of a metal spoon.

Transfer the sauce to a container, cover, and refrigerate overnight.

A serving of sauce is 3 tablespoons; ¾ cup of sauce will serve 4 people. Before serving, pour the sauce into a pan and rewarm over medium heat. Strain the sauce into a clean pan and keep warm over low heat.

# PAN SAUCE/ AU POIVRE

A steak covered in pepper sauce is the quintessential French bistro dish. One of my first memories of Paris in the '70s was walking down the Champs-Élysées at lunchtime and seeing every bistro crowded with businessmen, all of them eating steak au poivre with *pommes frites* and a glass of Beaujolais. The air just wafted with the scent of pepper and beef. If you consider yourself a good cooker of meat, you have to know how to do a steak au poivre.

A pan sauce can't be made completely ahead of time; it requires the cooking of the meat itself to provide the integral flavoring. It's a classic, fundamental technique, though, that should be in every home cook's arsenal. At Knife, we make the pan sauce au poivre—the classic peppery pan sauce from France (*poivre* is French for "pepper")—but you can use the technique with shallots, garlic, mustard, cognac, or whatever you want. You don't even have to use beef; you can do this with a pork chop or a chicken breast.

You can use any cut of steak you want—but I tailored this recipe for a flat iron, as it works perfectly when I'm cooking in a pan at home. At Knife, we use a strip steak for steak au poivre and serve it with *frites*, as the French do at pretty much every bistro. The cracked black pepper is strong, but cooking tempers it, allowing its sweetness to come out and harmonize with the meat.

Pan basting, or *poêlé*, comes into play here, as we like to get the salt and pepper that came into the pan on the steak back into the butter. As a rule, I only use butter because of how the fat distributes heat and binds with the meat juices. Also, I only make pan sauces in the stainless steel pan, because it's nonreactive and clean. I would not suggest making the sauce in the carbon steel pan, because the heat is a little too intense and can burn the ingredients.

While the meat rests, use the same pan to make the sauce, making sure to pour out the fat before starting the sauce. Some people like to finish the sauce with butter, but I'm getting more health conscious these days, so I skip it. I've given instructions for cooking a single steak, but the sauce recipe makes enough for 4–6. If you're not going to use it all at once, the sauce will keep for two days, covered, in the refrigerator, and can be reheated gently over low heat.

SERVES: 1, WITH EXTRA SAUCE

**1 flat iron steak, about 10 ounces**

**½ plus ⅛ teaspoon kosher salt**

**1 teaspoon freshly ground black pepper**

**¾ teaspoon butter**

FOR THE AU POIVRE SAUCE:

**1 tablespoon coarsely ground black pepper**

**1 heaping tablespoon Dijon mustard**

**¼ cup brandy**

**1 cup bordelaise sauce (see page 81)**

**½ cup heavy cream, plus 1–2 tablespoons additional, if needed**

**1 tablespoon green peppercorns in brine, drained, optional**

Season the steak evenly on both sides with ½ teaspoon of the salt and ½ teaspoon of the pepper.

In a stainless steel pan over very high heat, cook the butter until it gets brown. In French cooking, it's called *noisette*, which is French for "hazelnut." That's the color you want the butter to be.

Place the steak in the pan and make sure the entire surface makes contact with the butter. Cook the steak for 4–5 minutes, basting the meat once or twice with the juices and fat in the pan. Turn the steak and cook the other side. Using a digital thermometer, test the meat; you want it to read between 125–128 degrees F. Put the meat on a plate and let it rest for 5 minutes for a perfectly medium-rare steak.

Pour out the butter and fat, leaving the brown bits behind.

Add the coarsely ground black pepper and mustard to the pan and whisk to combine, picking up the brown bits from the bottom of the pan. Add the brandy and pull the pan off the heat unless you like high drama. Turn the flame to very low and whisk in the bordelaise sauce until you have a homogeneous sauce.

Whisk in the heavy cream; the sauce should be a light brown, like the color of suede. Add the remaining ⅛ teaspoon of salt and ½ teaspoon black pepper, and whisk to combine.

Add the green peppercorns, if using, and stir to combine. Turn the heat to medium and let the sauce cook. It should bubble a little around the edges of the pan, but it should not boil. Cook for 15–20 minutes, until the sauce is thick enough to coat the back of the spoon. If the sauce gets too dark, you can whisk in another tablespoon or two of cream.

Slice the steak and place it on a plate. Pour the sauce over and serve.

# BÉARNAISE SAUCE

Béarnaise is my all-time favorite sauce. I'm not a big sauce-on-steak person, but the original time I tasted properly made béarnaise sauce at Club Pierre, when Pierre first made it for me, a light went on. And it's never gone off. Nowadays, I'm still a stickler for béarnaise sauce, and when my cooks get it even slightly wrong, I make them toss it out and start over again.

Tart, tangy béarnaise is a vehicle for tarragon's pungent flavor. It's a derivative of hollandaise, one of France's "mother sauces." Both are emulsions of butter and egg yolks, but hollandaise is much plainer, while béarnaise is flavored with tarragon and vinegar and shallots. Making it used to require a lot of whisking over a steamy water bath until the eggs got to 135 degrees F. But with the modern food processor, this is no longer necessary, and making the sauce is a breeze. The acidic balance is the key to this sauce, as the recipe follows a basic ratio of 2 to 1, wine to vinegar. Use a decent white wine, not some sort of designated "cooking wine" from a grocery store. I finish with parsley and chives to balance out the potent note of tarragon. For me, a little Tabasco sauce subs for ground black pepper, whose grains have no place in my smooth, creamy sauce.

You may not want to use it only for steak; béarnaise goes deliciously with just about anything: fish, asparagus, chicken.

It will also keep for a couple of days, covered, in the refrigerator and can be gently reheated over low heat or in a double boiler. If the sauce breaks—which can happen if the butter gets too hot or the sauce gets too hot when you're reheating it—don't panic. Add 2 tablespoons of lukewarm water to a large bowl. Slowly stream in the sauce, whisking constantly, and the sauce should come together.

Using 1 pound of butter will make a little more than 2 cups of clarified butter. If you have any left over after you finished the recipe, it will keep, covered, in the refrigerator, almost indefinitely. Use it to scramble or fry eggs, or sauté meats or vegetables.

SERVES: 6–8

1 pound butter

¼ cup finely chopped shallots

½ cup dry white wine

¼ cup white wine vinegar

2 tablespoons plus 1½ teaspoons chopped tarragon

⅛ teaspoon freshly cracked black pepper, or 2 black peppercorns

3 egg yolks

1 tablespoon plus 1½ teaspoons finely chopped tarragon

1 tablespoon finely chopped chives

1½ teaspoons finely chopped parsley

½ teaspoon kosher salt

¼ teaspoon Tabasco

¼–½ teaspoon fresh lemon juice

In a heavy-bottomed saucepan over medium-low heat, melt the butter. As the butter melts, carefully skim off the white foam that rises to the top. When the butter is melted and all the foam has been skimmed off, there will be a layer of white sediment (milk solids) at the bottom

of the pan. Carefully pour the clarified butter through a strainer lined with cheesecloth into a measuring cup and keep warm.

Place the shallots, wine, vinegar, tarragon, and pepper or peppercorns in a nonreactive saucepan. Turn the heat to medium and cook the mixture, uncovered, until almost all the liquid is gone; you should have a little less than 2 teaspoons left. It will smell almost unpleasantly pungent.

Place the hot mixture in the bowl of a food processor. Add the egg yolks and start the machine. With the machine running, add 2 cups of the warm butter, ¼ cup at time, and process until the mixture is smooth and emulsified. Turn off the machine; the sauce should coat the back of a metal spoon.

Pour the sauce through a fine-mesh strainer into a bowl and discard the solids left in the strainer. Stir in the finely chopped tarragon, chives, parsley, salt, Tabasco, and lemon juice.

# CHIMI-CHURRI

I've always been suspicious of the Americanized Brazilian steakhouse concept of all-you-can-eat chunks of overcooked beef on a skewer. But, thankfully, it was at one of these temples to beef that I was introduced to the tangy, savory magic of chimichurri. There are many versions of chimichurri, the great sauce of Argentina and Brazil, and they're all tangy, bright, and irresistible not only on fire-roasted steak but anything pulled off the grill, from shrimp and chicken to lamb and pork. I like to use a fresh jalapeño for a peppery zing.

Use a nice, balanced French red wine vinegar, which I find are the best for cooking in general. I use a spicy, herbaceous Ligurian olive oil. If you prefer a milder flavor you can use a 75/25 blend of canola oil and extra-virgin olive oil (75 percent canola oil and 25 percent extra-virgin olive oil). Sometimes this sauce is served chunky, but I like to purée it in a blender for a smooth, creamy texture. With chimichurri and salsa verde (see page 91), allow the sauce to sit for an hour or two before serving, as the flavors round out and coalesce beautifully with a little time. I like to serve chimichurri especially with the leaner cuts of beef, as they benefit from the additional oil and the tanginess.

SERVES: 6–8
(Maybe up to 10 if you don't use a lot. I do.)

3 cloves garlic, peeled and stem ends removed

2 jalapeño peppers, seeded, cored, and ribs removed

½ cup packed parsley leaves

½ cup packed mint leaves

½ cup packed cilantro leaves

2 tablespoons red wine vinegar

2 tablespoons fresh lemon juice

¾ teaspoon kosher salt

½ teaspoon freshly ground black pepper

½ cup canola oil

½ cup extra-virgin olive or 75/25 canola/olive oil blend (see headnote), plus additional if needed

Put the garlic, jalapeños, parsley, mint, cilantro, vinegar, lemon juice, salt, pepper, and oils in the jar of a blender and cover.

Turn the blender on low, gradually increasing the speed to high. Check the mixture after about 30 seconds and scrape down the container. You want a nice creamy texture, like pesto, without chunks of jalapeño. If you need to continue blending, do it in short bursts so you don't heat the chimichurri. If the mixture is too thick, add a little more olive oil or canola/olive oil blend.

Taste and adjust the seasoning. Transfer the chimichurri to a bowl, cover, and set aside at room temperature for an hour or two. The acid in the vinegar and lemon juice will "cook" the herbs, and the flavors will bloom and meld.

# SALSA VERDE

This salsa verde is a Mediterranean version, not the Mexican one with tomatillos. Like chimichurri, it provides a brash, brilliant, complex flavor to meat, fish—anything. We even toss it with our fries. The tang comes from garlic, capers, and anchovies—basically a direct transfusion of umami. Parsley is the traditional herb ingredient that makes it *verde*, but I like to buff up the complexity by using cilantro and mint as well. In this case, I think it works best to use a good Italian extra-virgin olive oil, but the sauce will still be good if you want to cut the olive oil with something like canola oil. It's important that you put all the ingredients into the blender at the same time so you don't have to blend and blend, the action of which can damage the olive oil and create heat that will cook the herbs.

SERVES: 6–8
(Maybe up to 10 if you don't use a lot. I do.)

3 cloves garlic, peeled

10 white anchovy fillets in oil

¼ cup small nonpareil capers, drained but not rinsed

½ cup packed cilantro leaves

½ cup packed parsley leaves

½ cup packed mint leaves

1 tablespoon plus ¾ teaspoon fresh lemon juice

¾ teaspoon kosher salt

1 teaspoon freshly ground black pepper

⅓ cup canola oil

1 cup extra-virgin olive oil

Put the garlic, anchovies, capers, cilantro, parsley, mint, ¾ teaspoon of the lemon juice, ½ teaspoon of the salt, ½ teaspoon of the pepper, canola oil, and olive oil in the jar of a blender and cover.

Turn the blender on low, gradually increasing the speed to high. Check the mixture after about 30 seconds and scrape down the container. You want a nice creamy texture, like pesto.

Taste, and add the remaining 1 tablespoon lemon juice, ¼ teaspoon salt, and ½ teaspoon pepper. Blend on the lowest speed to incorporate.

# COMPOUND BUTTERS

I'm different from many people in that I'm not a big fan of pouring straight butter over steak. But I can admit that the leaner cuts like the flat iron, culotte, or the chuck flap can occasionally use a little boost in fat content, and a compound butter is an excellent solution. It's just herbs or other flavorings mixed into softened butter, after which the mixture is recooled. The butter hardens in the refrigerator in whatever shape you've given it and can be easily sliced or scooped onto a hot steak just before serving, over which it promptly melts, spreading its flavor accents in a gloss of buttery richness.

A good technique for shaping the butter is to scoop it on a sheet of parchment paper in a long mound and roll the paper like you are making a sushi roll until the butter forms a nice cylinder, about the diameter of a quarter. Chill it down in the fridge until it's hardened, and then you can just cut a slab off the end and throw away the paper wrapping, and the butter will melt all over the steak. Once made, it will last for weeks in the fridge. ★

Kimchi Butter

# KIMCHI BUTTER

If you're not familiar with kimchi, it's Korea's answer to sauerkraut—naturally fermented cabbage, sometimes fermented for over a year—with spicy peppers and all sorts of other umami-rich flavorings. It's bold, spicy, tangy, and delicious. We had developed our kimchi butter to go with prawns and lobster, but the revelation of its use with meat came a couple of years ago when I was asked by my dear, departed friend Josh Ozersky to provide a dish for an event called Meatopia. They provided the meat for us, which that year was unfortunately a really uninspiring lamb. So I went looking for some inspirationally powerful flavors in Koreatown and ended up buying some Korean red pepper for a rub.

Lo and behold, the next day, this uninspiring lamb had turned into the most delicate spiced lamb. So I brought out the kimchi butter to serve with it, and it was a remarkable combination. Instead of revealing ourselves as culinary geniuses, however, I think we just learned that kimchi butter goes with everything. My favorite compound butter, this adds the spicy, pungent element from kimchi and an enticing red color to a lovely infusion of buttery richness. No need to age and ferment your kimchi for months or a year for this. You can find jars of kimchi concentrate, a powerful flavor extract, at most any Korean or Asian market.

YIELD: 3½ CUPS

**2 cups beurre monté (see page 225)**
**1½ cups kimchi concentrate**
**1/16 teaspoon freshly ground black pepper (optional)**

In a saucepan over medium heat, warm the beurre monté. Add the kimchi base and whisk vigorously to blend. Add the black pepper if you want a bit more punch.

# ANCHOVY BUTTER

Anchovy butter is the simplest way to get a little surf-and-turf vibe for your steak. Anchovies are packed with umami, and so is steak. Thus, melting a compound anchovy butter on a hot steak simply amps up the deep, savory deliciousness. Don't worry about a fishy-tasting piece of beef. Use white anchovies packed in oil, which are mild, not like the salty ones that come in tins. White anchovies contribute a funky element that's offset by the citrusy bite of lemon juice.

It may be easier to make this in two batches. Be patient; it takes time to get the mixed butter completely smooth. Anchovy butter will keep almost indefinitely in the freezer. Cut off what you need when you need it and melt over the steak of your choice.

YIELD: 2½ CUPS

1 pound unsalted butter, cut into chunks

2 tablespoons minced shallot

½ cup packed white anchovies in olive oil

½ teaspoon kosher salt

½ teaspoon Tabasco

2 tablespoons plus 1½ teaspoons fresh lemon juice

Place ½ pound of the butter, the shallots, and the anchovies in the bowl of a food processor fitted with the steel blade and process until blended.

With the machine running, add the remaining butter, a chunk at a time, until it is all incorporated and completely smooth and creamy, stopping the machine to scrape down the bowl occasionally. Add the salt, Tabasco, and lemon juice, scrape down the sides, and continue to process until completely smooth. This will take at least 10–15 minutes.

THE COMPLETE MEAT

Pork Chops and Applesauce

It's important to have a go-to dish—something delicious that you've practiced and know you can make with 100 percent success. So in this chapter, which looks beyond steak, I give some advice for understanding and selecting the right kind of meats from the other major meat groups and then offer a go-to recipe for that meat.

The first section is on lamb, an underrated meat that Americans don't eat enough of. The go-to recipe regards a skill every cook should have—how to prepare a basic rack of lamb. It's classic, delicious, and always makes an impressive presentation.

After lamb, I briefly discuss pork. Though for a time pork farmers liked to bill it as "the other white meat," the best pork isn't really that. It's somewhere between white and red meat, with a flavor all its own. The go-to recipe for pork is a simple way to cook chops without drying them out and then pairing them with a beautiful preparation of apples, whose sweetness makes a fabulous accompaniment.

Poultry is a big part of every carnivore's life, and it's good to have a couple of killer recipes in your back pocket to get the most out of a bird, be it chicken, duck, quail, or turkey. In this section, I offer go-to recipes for the two most common birds we regularly see in stores today: chicken and duck. The chicken recipe is my version of one of America's finest chicken preparations, whole roasted chicken; it's a good one to have in your back pocket, as everyone who tastes it loves this dish. Duck confit is so tasty and so foolproof that I think every home chef should know how to make it. It takes some time to prepare, but it is otherwise as exceedingly simple in execution as it is big in flavor and satisfaction.

Next, I go back to the beloved cow, but not for steak. Rather, this recipe is for a slow-cooked piece of beef that renders exquisite flavor and texture. You can slow cook beef in a number of ways, from roasting to braising to stewing. But for this, I offer another, more modern technique that yields impressive results: sous vide. The sous vide technique allows you to cook what would otherwise be a tough piece of meat into a delicious, melt-in-your-mouth tender piece that can then be seared and served almost like a steak—an amazing hybrid of slow cooked and quick seared.

Finally, each of these go-to dishes requires no fancy skills to accomplish, and will reward cooking again and again. That's the Complete Meat.

## LAMB

I have a real fondness for lamb, as there were a couple of years when I was a kid that it was all I wanted to eat. Lamb is also a great red-meat alternative to beef. It's got a different and often much more intense flavor than beef. Just as a hunk of beef, a rack or leg of lamb makes an impressively rich, savory centerpiece to any table. Another great thing about lamb: It holds its own beautifully with any rich, red wine.

When it comes to lamb, there's always the one basic choice: Foreign or domestic? Imported lamb tends to come from Australia and New Zealand, while the most commonly found domestic lamb is from Colorado or the high rangelands of other western states. My preference is always for Colorado lamb.

Aussie and Kiwi lamb can be tasty, but it tends to come from animals that are generally raised for wool (the merino breed). They also tend to be grass fed their entire lives and are slaughtered when quite young, at around six or seven months of age. The result is pungently grassy-flavored lamb, whose cuts are small and meat is lean. It can be delicious if you like very herbal, grassy lamb, but the size of the cuts and the toughness are the drawbacks. Funnily enough, the imported lamb is usually cheaper than domestic lamb. Both Southern Hemisphere countries have more sheep than people, leading to giant lamb and sheep industries, built for export. Our domestic lamb industry is relatively small.

Colorado lamb is very different from imported lamb. It comes from different breeds and is often grain finished before slaughter at an older age. The resulting meat is mellower tasting, marbled for a tender texture, and comes in more generously sized cuts, making for a fuller portion. For me, Colorado lamb is the quintessential balance of fat, true lamb flavor, and meatiness. ★

Rack of Colorado Lamb, Mustard, Garlic, and Herb Crust

# RACK OF COLORADO LAMB, MUSTARD, GARLIC & HERB CRUST

I've been making this version of rack of lamb for over thirty years. It was taught to me by Chef Oliver Smith, who was the saucier who worked under star chef Masa Kobayashi at the famed New York restaurant Le Plaisir.

Based on classic French technique and taste, the preparation is still one of the most delicious ways to enjoy lamb. The French term for this style is *persillade*, which just means a parsley-based seasoning (*persil* is "parsley" in French). In France, parsley is often found accompanying lamb, because its strong herbal flavor both complements and tempers the strong taste of lamb. (In English food, lamb and mutton are often served with a condiment made from mint, an even more aggressive flavor than parsley. This is probably because mutton—the meat from adult sheep—is even sharper tasting than lamb.)

In this dish, I supplement the parsley with bread crumbs as well as powerful notes from thyme, rosemary leaves, and garlic—all these flavors are terrific with lamb.

Most butchers sell rack of lamb that's been frenched (cleaned of the fat and meat in between the rib bones). If it's not been cleaned up by the butcher, it's easy enough to do yourself. Just pull the fat cap off with your hands and with a paring knife clean the extraneous fat and flap of thin meat off the bones so that they're bare all the way to the meat, to create those little lamb "lollipops." Cut off the muscle that runs along the chine at the bottom of the rack. Trim any excess fat off the back of the rack, but don't cut it off completely.

You can cook a rack at any size you want, but I recommend two bones per person unless you're really hungry. Later, when I roast the lamb, I wrap the bones in foil to preserve their lovely whiteness and to keep them from getting too brittle—this is just cosmetic.

SERVES: 2

**4 thin slices commercial white bread, crusts removed**

**2½ tablespoons packed parsley leaves**

**Leaves from 1 stalk thyme**

**Leaves from 1 small branch rosemary**

**3 medium garlic cloves**

**¾ teaspoon kosher salt**

**¾ teaspoon freshly ground black pepper**

**1 (4-rib) rack of lamb**

**1½ teaspoons extra-virgin olive oil, plus additional for drizzling**

**1 tablespoon Dijon mustard**

Preheat the oven to 425 degrees F.

Put the bread, parsley, thyme, rosemary, garlic, ¼ teaspoon of the salt and ¼ teaspoon of the pepper into the bowl of a food processor fitted with the steel blade. Pulse until you have a green, moist, perfumed mixture of fine herbed bread crumbs.

Cover the exposed lamb bones with foil. Season the lamb with the remaining ½ teaspoon salt and ½ teaspoon pepper.

Heat the olive oil in an ovenproof sauté pan over high heat. Place the rack, fat side down, in the skillet and sear just until the fat is caramelized. Quickly sear the sides.

Coat the top of the lamb with the mustard. Sprinkle the top of the lamb with the bread crumb mixture, shake off the excess, and lightly pat the crumbs into the mustard. Repeat the process until no mustard is visible. You want a light, even coating.

Wipe out the sauté pan and place the rack, coated-side up, in the pan. Rest the bones on the edge to stabilize the rack. Drizzle with olive oil and put the pan in the oven.

Roast the lamb for 16–18 minutes. Remove the pan from the oven and let the lamb rest for 8–10 minutes.

Transfer the rack to a cutting board and remove the foil. With the crust facing you, hold the rack by the bones and, with a sharp knife, cut between the chops, pressing down and taking the knife in one direction, creating four lamb chops.

Pork Chops and Applesauce

# PORK

The pig is a gift. I love pork for its versatility, but it challenges the chef, as it's more technical than other meats because you can use every part of the animal. You can really eat the entire beast: the liver makes excellent pâté; the hooves make gelée; the tails, ears, and skin can be fried into cracklings.

The major downside of pork in the last twenty years is the decline of both flavor and fat. How is it that the beef industry has been breeding for marbling, yet the goal of the pork industry has been to create the leanest, most flavorless meat on the planet? It's disappointing on so many levels. The goal was evidently to create "the other white meat" that could compete with boneless, skinless chicken breasts for the stomachs and wallets of the body-obsessed Lean Cuisine generation. What's sad is that this direction perverted the pig from its nature as an animal that ate a diverse diet and developed deep flavor and significant fat content.

Happily, that's coming back to some degree in the form of the heritage breeds we find today. But the damage has been done: An entire generation of people don't know what real pork tastes like and, if they had it, would probably find it too "porky." When you can find it, order heritage pork breeds—Berkshire, Duroc, Red Wattle, to name a few—at restaurants and to cook at home. ★

# PORK CHOPS & APPLE— SAUCE

I love pork belly, I love ribs, I love ham. But there's no quicker way to get a pork fix than the chop. My mother used to take very thin rib pork chops and cook them in a hot pan. But they were so thin, she'd always overcook them, and they'd be tough and dry. I like to cook pork like I cook steak—it should be pink inside. We needn't fear trichinosis. If you're using good-quality pork, there's no fear of it. Even the USDA changed its stance (which always defaults to food safety over deliciousness), issuing a bulletin that it's okay to have pink pork. As the National Pork Board explains on its website: "The widespread adoption of improved feeding practices and high levels of biosecurity and hygiene have virtually eliminated the presence of trichinae in the United States." So there you have it—with confidence, serve it nice and pink for optimal tenderness and flavor!

When I think of apples and pork, I think German and my own Eastern European heritage. The fatty mildness of pork makes it an ideal match for the acidic sweetness of the apple, which creates a natural agrodolce (an Italian sweet-and-sour sauce). I wouldn't serve applesauce with beef, but with pork it's natural.

In this dish, the applesauce—like a sip of wine—is a palate cleanser. It makes you want to go back for more. I like a very silky, refined applesauce. The mixture of Granny Smith and a sweeter variety provides the perfect tart/sweet balance. This stuff is so delicious that people can't believe there are only three ingredients.

Tahitian vanilla has a fruity, floral aroma and a rich flavor. It's what I prefer, but use whatever vanilla beans are available to you. Just don't use vanilla extract; it doesn't work in this recipe. Wash and dry the vanilla bean when you're done and stick it in a jar of sugar to make vanilla sugar. It's not necessary to coat the apples in lemon juice to keep them from browning. If they brown, it's fine; you're going to be cooking them anyway. When you're cooking the applesauce, leave a wooden spoon in the middle of the pot to diffuse some of the heat. It allows the apples to cook more evenly and reminds you to stir.

Don't crowd the pork chops in the pan. If you have a skillet big enough to cook all the chops at the same time, great. Otherwise, cook them two at a time. Don't overcook the pork unless you like dry, tasteless meat—145 degrees is hot enough to kill anything that can hurt you and still give you a juicy, tender chop.

SERVES: 4

FOR THE APPLESAUCE:

**3 Granny Smith apples**

**3 Gala or Fuji apples**

**10 ounces unsweetened apple juice, like Martinelli's**

**½ vanilla bean, preferably Tahitian, split and scraped of its seeds; discard the seeds**

FOR THE PORK CHOPS:

**4 (8–10-ounce) pork loin chops**

**Kosher salt and freshly ground white pepper**

**2 tablespoons 75/25 canola/olive oil blend (see page 88)**

**Make the applesauce:** Peel and core the apples, then cut them into ½-inch cubes. You should end up with about 1 quart tightly packed apples.

Put the apples, apple juice, and vanilla bean in a nonreactive saucepan over medium-low heat. Stir often, turning the top to the bottom as the apples begin to cook down. Simmer gently for 45 minutes to an hour until the apple cubes have mostly broken down into applesauce consistency, soft and without too much excess liquid. Remove the vanilla bean.

Remove the pan from the heat and let cool slightly. You can use a handheld blender and purée the applesauce right in the pot, or put it in a blender and blend until smooth.

**Make the pork chops:** Heat a cast-iron or carbon steel pan over medium heat for 3–4 minutes.

While the pan is heating, season the chops liberally with salt and white pepper.

Add a tablespoon of oil to the pan for two pork chops.

Cook the pork chops for 5–7 minutes per side. As the fat renders out into the pan, baste the juices and fat back over the chops, *poêlé*-style.

When the chops are well browned and have reached an internal temperature of 145 degrees F, remove the chops from the pan and let rest, uncovered, for 5 minutes.

**To serve:** Slice the meat off the bone into ¼-inch-thick slices. Serve alongside a healthy dollop of applesauce.

# BIRDS

When it comes to poultry, I have mixed opinions. Some birds I love, some I don't. I can never get excited about quail—too many of them in Texas, and most people overcook them dreadfully. And I could altogether do without the turkey.

However, I worship at the altar of the chicken. Still to this day, I eat roast chicken once a week. It's the easiest and most natural thing to cook. When buying chickens, stay away from anything commercial. Try to find something local. They need to be free range and eat organically. There's nothing better than a 3–3.5 pound roasted local chicken, cavity stuffed with aromatics like thyme, lemon, garlic, bay leaf, and rosemary, and then coated in olive oil, salt, and pepper. Despite what they tell you, you never have to truss the whole chicken. Just tie the legs together to close up the cavity, but not so tightly that the legs touch the breast. I also cut the tips of the wings off. That's all there is to it.

Then there's duck, which, in terms of versatility and flavor, is as magical as the pig. There are two schools to roasting a duck—slow and fast. My mother went slow. She would roast it at 275 degrees F for 5–6 hours, basting it with its own juices. The French method of roasting the duck is to go higher, at 350 for 2.5–3 hours. The most foolproof way to cook a duck is to confit it in its own fat.

On page 111, I give you my version of an iconic chicken recipe and, on page 115, a wonderful, timeless preparation for duck confit. Both are perfect go-to recipes, and mastering them will make you happy for the rest of your life. ★

# WHOLE ROAST CHICKEN
## WITH PANZANELLA SALAD À LA ZUNI CAFÉ

We routinely offer one special chicken dish on the menu for a very specific reason: to honor the late Judy Rodgers, whom I encountered over several decades in France, New York, and San Francisco. She was a very strong-willed and determined person, and I was the same. We had great respect for each other. Judy died in 2013 after a battle with the exceedingly rare cancer of the appendix.

This roasted chicken is a version of the dish she created and made famous at San Francisco's Zuni Café. It's one of the iconic chicken preparations of the world, and if you go to San Francisco, a meal at Zuni for the famous roast chicken for two is a must. Be sure to leave enough time. The dish takes between fifty minutes and an hour to cook, and the restaurant doesn't take advance orders, which is brilliant in all sorts of ways. First, the extra time is good for the restaurant, because in the hour you're waiting for your chicken, you're going to want to order wine and a whole host of starters, from the oysters to the Caesar to the shoestring fries. It's likewise a boon for the diner for all the above reasons—the oysters, Caesar, and wine list are all great.

The pairing of a perfectly roasted chicken's juicy interior and its crispy skin just kissed with smoke from the wood-fired oven with a bread salad and seasonal, bitter greens is brilliant. The day-old, absorbent cubed bread is tossed in the pan drippings and vinegar, and the whole shebang is tossed together and served in a shallow bowl.

A critic once dinged me for the messiness of presentation in this chicken, which only furthered my mistrust and disappointment in the modern American restaurant critic. The critic—in Dallas—must have been wholly oblivious to the reference of this dish, which at Zuni is served as a jumble. Criticizing its presentation is like giving demerits to a pasta carbonara for including pork or a salade Niçoise for being composed—it fails to comprehend an essential nature of the dish. Okay, rant over.

Here's our quicker take on the Zuni roast chicken. One thing to note: We do things a little differently at Knife than they do at Zuni Café; we don't salt the chicken ahead of time, and we make the salad with wild arugula (also called rocket), sherry vinegar, chicken drippings, and shallots. Use any good crusty, open-crumbed, chewy, peasant-style bread for the salad except sourdough. You can toast the bread earlier in the day and assemble the salad while the chicken is roasting.

SERVES: 4–6

(recipe continues)

**FOR THE CHICKEN:**

**1 chicken, 2¾–3½ pounds**

**4 (½-inch) sprigs fresh thyme, marjoram, rosemary, or sage**

**2–2½ teaspoons kosher salt (¾ teaspoon per pound of chicken)**

**¼ teaspoon freshly ground black pepper**

**FOR THE SALAD:**

**8 ounces day-old peasant-style bread**

**½ cup mild olive oil**

**1½ tablespoons plus 1 teaspoon sherry vinegar**

**Kosher salt and freshly ground black pepper**

**1 tablespoon dried currants**

**1 tablespoon warm water**

**2 cloves garlic, slivered**

**½ cup very thinly sliced shallots**

**2 tablespoons chicken stock or lightly salted water**

**A few handfuls of wild arugula, well washed and dried**

**Make the chicken:** Preheat the oven to 475 degrees F. Position the rack in the center of the oven.

Clean the chicken, removing any extra lumps of fat or excess skin. Pat the chicken dry with paper towels, inside and out.

Slide a finger under the skin on each side of the breast, making two pockets. Carefully use your fingertip to loosen a pocket on the outside of thickest part of the thigh. Be careful not to break the skin. Put a sprig of herb into each pocket.

Season the chicken with the salt and pepper, seasoning the meaty parts of the breast and legs more heavily. Sprinkle a little salt on the interior backbone. With kitchen shears, snip off the tips of the wings so they don't burn in the oven.

Place in a shallow roasting pan just big enough to hold the chicken or in a 10-inch ovenproof skillet over medium heat. Place the chicken breast-side up in the pan; you should hear it sizzle. Place the pan in the oven; the chicken should start sizzling and browning within 20 minutes. If it doesn't, or it begins to burn instead of blister, or the fat starts smoking, you will have to adjust your oven up or down 25 degrees F.

After 30 minutes, turn the chicken breast-side down and cook for another 10–20 minutes (depending on the size of your bird) and then cook breast-side up for another 5–10 minutes to recrisp the skin. The total cooking time will be 45–60 minutes.

**Make the salad:** Make sure there is space to position a rack in the top third of the oven.

Cut the bread into several big chunks. Remove the bottom crust and most of the top and side crusts and reserve for another purpose (like bread crumbs or croutons).

Toss the bread with a tablespoon or two of the olive oil and put on a baking sheet. Bake for a minute or two until golden brown and crisp, and then turn and bake the other side. Trim any charred bread, and then tear the bread into a combination of 2–3 inch chunks, bite-sized pieces, and crumbs. You should have about 4 cups total. Place the bread in a large serving bowl.

In a small bowl, combine 4 tablespoons of the olive oil with the vinegar and add salt and pepper to taste. Pour about ¼ cup of the dressing over the bread; the bread won't be

(recipe continues)

evenly dressed. Taste a small, more saturated piece and adjust the seasoning if necessary.

Put the currants in a small bowl and pour 1 teaspoon of the sherry vinegar and the warm water over. Set aside.

Heat a tablespoon of olive oil in a skillet over medium heat and add the garlic and shallots. Cook, stirring constantly, until the garlic and shallots are softened; don't let them color. Add to the bread and toss. Drain the currants and toss with the bread. Dribble the chicken stock or water over the salad and toss. Taste a piece of bread and adjust the seasoning by adding salt, pepper, or additional vinegar to taste.

Place the bread in a baking dish, cover loosely with foil, and place in the oven while the chicken is breast-side up for the last time.

**To serve:** Remove the chicken from the oven and turn off the heat; leave the baking dish in for another 5 minutes.

Put the chicken on a plate and pour off the fat from the pan, leaving the rest of the drippings behind. Add a tablespoon of water to the pan and swirl it around. Cut the skin between the chicken breast and thighs and add those juices to the drippings. Let the chicken rest in a warm place while you finish the bread salad and put the serving platter into the oven. Remove the bread.

Skim any fat from the juices in the roasting pan and place over medium heat. Add any more juices that have come out of the chicken and bring to a simmer. Scrape any hardened drippings from the bottom of the pan.

Put the bread salad into a bowl. Drizzle with a tablespoon of drippings and toss. Add the arugula, a tablespoon of the vinaigrette, and toss again.

Cut the chicken into serving pieces. Remove the platter from the oven, arrange the bread salad on the platter and the chicken over the bread salad.

# SPICE— CURED DUCK CONFIT

In 1982, when I dropped out of NYU to go La Varenne, I didn't even know what duck confit was. It was at that cooking school that I heard about duck confit, and I was instantly intrigued by the idea of cooking something entirely in its own fat.

To confit (*con-FEE*) is the ancient technique of cooking duck or goose in its own fat, resulting in an incredibly tender, flavorful meat whose skin will crisp up remarkably under high heat. For this recipe, I prefer to use the breed called Pekin duck, also known as Long Island duck, which tends to be tenderer. If you don't have access to Pekin duck, don't worry—any duck will work well.

The spice, sugar, and salt mixture is the dry cure, flavoring and tenderizing the duck at the same time. While you can render your own duck fat, it's much easier to buy a quart or two at a good butcher, liquefy it in a pot, and pour it over the duck.

Once you get the technique down, you can play around with the cure, trying different herbs and spices as long as the balance of sugar and salt remains palatable. Juniper berries make a fine addition to a cure, as do cardamom pods for something more exotic.

A cartouche is a makeshift drop lid, fashioned by cutting a piece of parchment paper to fit snugly inside the pot, resting directly on what you're cooking. It reduces evaporation, while simultaneously keeping the ingredients submerged.

You'll know the duck is finished when the meat has pulled back from the end of the drumstick, exposing the bone. Despite all the duck fat in the recipe, there's not that much in the dish because it's all been rendered out. Once it's cooled, you can use the gorgeous sweet-salty-spicy duck for any number of things. You can pull the meat and add it to a salad or make a pasta sauce out of it. Or, when it gets to room temperature, you can delicately pull the leg and thigh bones out of the meat, preserving the meat's shape, and fry the remaining piece in a pan with a little bit of duck fat over low heat. Cook it like this until the skin has become nice and crispy, and then serve the meat over some potatoes, polenta, or greens.

SERVES: 4

**4 duck legs**

**1 cup kosher salt**

**½ cup sugar**

**2 tablespoons freshly ground black pepper**

**1½ heaping tablespoons ground star anise**

**½ teaspoon ground cinnamon**

**2–3 sprigs fresh thyme**

**8 cloves garlic, peeled**

**2 quarts (32 ounces) rendered duck fat, warmed until pourable**

(recipe continues)

Remove any excess gobs of fat from the duck legs; discard the fat. Gently cover as much of the duck meat with the skin as possible.

In a bowl, place the salt, sugar, pepper, star anise, and cinnamon and mix well to combine. Holding each duck leg over a plate, liberally sprinkle the mixture over the entire surface of the duck and let the excess fall onto the plate. Don't press it into the skin. Cover a large plate or rimmed baking sheet with parchment or plastic wrap and place the duck legs, skin-side down, on the plate. Refrigerate, uncovered, for 24 hours, or up to, but no more than, 72 hours.

Preheat the oven to 250 degrees F.

Rinse the duck legs and pat dry. Place the legs skin-side down in a large, heavy-bottomed pot. Add the thyme and garlic, and pour the liquid duck fat over the duck legs. The fat should cover the legs completely.

Cut a circle of parchment paper large enough to fit inside the pot and cover the duck; press it gently over the duck. Cover the pot with foil or a tight-fitting lid.

Put the pot in the oven and cook for 2 hours and 15–20 minutes. Check occasionally to make sure the fat isn't boiling; if it is, turn the heat down.

Remove the pot from the oven and let cool. When the pot is at room temperature, it can be refrigerated or cooked immediately.

Remove the duck from the fat and gently pull on the thigh bone and drumstick. They should slip out easily. Gently pull the skin so it's flat over the meat so all the skin will make contact with the pan.

In a nonstick pan over medium heat, heat ½ tablespoon of the duck fat from the pot. Put the duck into the pan and turn the heat to very low. Cook until the skin is crisp and brittle and the meat warmed through.

## SLOW-COOKED BEEF

Being in Texas, I find myself often in the company of barbecue masters, whose specialty is slow-cooked beef. However, being a New Yorker, I learned barbecue from Jews and French people. If barbecue is all about cooking low and slow with smoke, the New York style is the same, minus the smoke. In fact, when we slow cook in the Knife kitchen, it's not uncommon for me to announce to the crew, "Get ready, we're making French barbecue today!"

Slow cooking is an art, and the cow provides so many wonderful cuts for this process—there's the oxtail, shank, and short rib, and tongue for braising. There's the rump for turning into roast beef. The brisket for barbecue or pastrami. Those are the classic methods of slow cooking. But in the last twenty years, a new method has emerged called sous vide. It allows you to do all kinds of new and interesting things, because it takes cooking to the lowest and the slowest.

I love to do this really interesting hybrid presentation of the short rib (the classic slow-cooking cut) that I want to share with you. It's a rather lengthy process, but the result brings you the depth and texture of the long, slow cook with the sizzle of a steak. I think it's pretty amazing. ★

Sous Vide Bone-In Short Rib Steak

# SOUS VIDE BONE–IN SHORT RIB STEAK

This is a little advanced for the home cook, but it's worth trying if you're into sous vide. Through the advancements of modern technology, sous vide has become highly affordable to do at home, and I predict in the years to come that sous vide equipment will be as common in modern kitchens as blenders and mixers. This new technology allows for some of the most demanding (or time-consuming) dishes on restaurant menus to be made at home. Here, you're basically cooking the meat in its own juices for a deep, pure, beefy flavor and a beautiful melt-in-your-mouth texture.

First, buy a full English short rib—it's the fourth, fifth, and sixth rib of the steer with the chuck flap left on. This is the whole rib; not like the crosscut short ribs you may be familiar with. You probably won't find this cut in the meat case at the supermarket; you'll need to ask the butcher to cut them for you. You can describe them as I did, or ask for cut 123A. Most people find it so impressively rich that one rib can easily satisfy two for dinner.

The meat cooks for three days but only to medium temperature. You can use plastic bags specially made for use with a sous vide machine, but a heavy-duty ziplock plastic bag is less expensive and just as effective. This is the miracle of sous vide: to be able to cook something to a certain temperature and then simply hold it there for days, breaking down tough muscle tissue without losing moisture or employing higher heat. After cooking the meat for 72 hours, there's not even a need to serve it right away. If you want to store it, run it under cold water for 10 minutes, and then put it in an ice bath to slowly chill it down. It can be stored after that for quite a while; just heat it back up to the original temperature in a water bath when you're ready to do the dish.

After the sous vide, sear it like a steak in the blue steel pan until we get the great browning as described in chapter 4, Steak. If the bone is too long for the pan, just carefully slice the meat off the bone and sear the meat like a boneless steak.

In the pan, *poêlé* the steak for excellent caramelization (see page 68). Let it rest for about 4–5 minutes. Then slice it crossways, against the grain. It literally melts in your mouth, while the browned meat gives a great texture like a wood fire, but without the smoke.

SERVES: 3–6

**1 English-cut short rib (see headnote)**

**1 tablespoon plus ½ teaspoon kosher salt**

**1 tablespoon plus ½ teaspoon freshly ground black pepper**

**2 tablespoons canola oil**

Separate the ribs by standing them on end and cutting straight down between the bones. Rub 1 tablespoon each of the salt and pepper into the meat, coating all the surfaces. If you have a bag that can hold all the ribs, great; otherwise, place each rib in an individual plastic bag, squeeze out all the air, and seal the bag.

Fill a pot or container that is large enough to hold all the ribs to three-quarters full of warm water. Attach the sous vide circulator, plug it in, and set it to 135 degrees F. Immerse the ribs and cook for 72 hours. When you take the ribs out, they'll be as tender as a baby's butt and will look like they've been cooked to a perfect medium rare to medium.

If you're not going to serve the ribs right away, run the bag under cold water for about 10 minutes, then leave in an ice bath for 45 minutes to an hour. Refrigerate the bags until you need them.

Otherwise, run the bags under cold water for 1–2 minutes. Carefully remove the ribs, leaving the juices in the bag. Discard the bag and juices.

Stand a rib on a cutting board and cut along the bone, following the natural curve of the ribs. The meat will just fall away from the bone. Season the ribs with the remaining ½ teaspoon salt and ½ teaspoon pepper.

In a cast-iron or blue steel pan over high heat, heat the canola oil. Sear a rib for about 20 seconds on all sides, basting with the oil and fat in the pan. You're just getting some texture and caramelization on the beef; don't cook it too long.

Transfer the rib to a plate and let it rest for 4–5 minutes. Repeat the process with the other ribs, depending on the number of servings you need.

Slice the rib across the grain and serve.

44 Farms Meatballs "Parmesan Style" and Spicy Marinara

## MEAT MEDLEY

Different kinds of meat don't necessarily need to always be kept separate; multiple proteins can work wonderfully in concert. We see this in many cultures, from the combination of shrimp and pork in a Vietnamese spring roll to the mix of duck and rabbit and pork in a French cassoulet to the simple act of putting bacon on a burger. One of my favorite combinations of different meats comes in Italian, Bolognese-style cooking, where a medley of pork, beef, and veal creates a complexity of flavor that adds real depth to the dish. ★

# 44 FARMS MEATBALLS "PARMESAN STYLE" & SPICY MARINARA

My love of the meatball comes from my mother, but my quest for the perfect meatball continues to this day. Over the years, I've had many, many good ones, but never the perfect one. For me, there are three basic characteristics of a proper meatball. The first is moisture content after cooking—it needs to be moist and tender. The second is structure—the interior must be a ground, textured meat (never puréed), but it needs to hold together as one entity. And the third basic characteristic is that the combination of textural integrity and moisture must produce a crisp exterior crust that contrasts with the moist interior. Such a meatball is very difficult to achieve, and this recipe is as close as I've come.

I use a combination of half sirloin and half dry-aged beef trimmings to make these meatballs at the restaurant, but all sirloin works well too. If you want to switch it up, substitute lamb shoulder for the sirloin. The meat and lardo should be ground together three times through the coarse plate of a meat grinder. If you don't want to do this yourself, ask your butcher to do it for you. Don't use the preground packages you find in the meat case.

The marinara sauce is quite flavorful. The recipe calls for Pomi chopped tomatoes. These have really great flavor, and I won't use anything else for this sauce. To make the sauce, use a nonreactive—stainless steel or copper—pot and a heatproof silicone or wooden spoon. Aluminum or other metals will affect the taste of the sauce, and not for the better. I leave the spoon or spatula in the sauce while it's cooking; it keeps the sauce from scorching. The deeply flavored oil skimmed from the sauce will keep indefinitely, covered, in the refrigerator. You can't cook with it (it's taken on too much water for that), but it can be used in salad dressings or to garnish risotto.

At Knife, the meatballs are an appetizer, so I don't serve them over pasta. But if that's your preference, go right ahead, as these can make an excellent main course too. I figure five meatballs per person served with ½ cup of sauce makes a fine entrée, and three meatballs served with ⅓ cup of sauce is an appetizer.

Start the sauce the day before you want to serve this; it has to sit overnight in the refrigerator. This recipe makes a lot, but I think it's nice to have extra. Leftovers will keep, stored separately or combined, in a covered container in the refrigerator for up to a week. Both sauce and meatballs freeze well.

SERVES: 8–10

2 cups 75/25 canola/olive oil blend
(see page 88)

3 large stalks rosemary

2 large sprigs thyme

1 medium carrot, peeled and coarsely chopped

1 medium Spanish onion, coarsely chopped

10–15 cloves garlic

1 bay leaf

2 (26.46-ounce) cartons Pomi chopped
tomatoes

1 tablespoon kosher salt

1 tablespoon finely ground black pepper

1 teaspoon red pepper flakes

FOR THE MEATBALLS:

2 slices white bread, like Pepperidge Farm,
crusts removed

¼ cup whole milk

1 cup extra-virgin olive oil

1 small yellow onion, finely diced

3 cloves garlic, thinly sliced

½ pound pork shoulder

½ pound veal

1 pound well-marbled sirloin

¼ pound ground lardo

1 egg

¼ cup packed basil leaves

¼ cup packed oregano leaves

1 teaspoon red pepper flakes

1½ tablespoons kosher salt

¾ cup fresh finely grated Parmesan cheese

Chopped parsley, for garnish

**Make the spicy marinara sauce:** In a large, heavy-bottomed nonreactive pot over medium-high heat, heat the blended oil. Then add the rosemary, thyme, carrot, onion, garlic, and bay leaf. Cook for 20–25 minutes, until the vegetables are caramelized. Remove the pot from the heat.

Put the tomatoes in a large, heavy-bottomed nonreactive pot set over low heat. Immediately strain the oil through a fine-mesh strainer into the tomatoes and discard the solids. Mix the oil and tomatoes, and add the salt, black pepper, and red pepper flakes. Leave a wooden spoon or heatproof spatula in the sauce. Cook, stirring occasionally, for 35–45 minutes. Remove the pot from the heat, and when the sauce has cooled slightly, pour it into containers. Cover and refrigerate overnight.

When you remove the containers from the refrigerator, the oil will have risen to the top. Skim off as much of the oil from the sauce as you can and reserve.

**Make the meatballs:** Place the bread in a small bowl and pour the milk over. Set aside.

In a skillet over medium-high heat, heat 2 tablespoons of olive oil and add the onion and garlic. Cook until the onion is translucent and soft, about 5–7 minutes. Let cool.

(recipe continues)

If you are grinding the meat yourself, put the pork, veal, sirloin, and lardo through the coarse plate of a meat grinder into a large bowl. If you are using butcher-ground meat, put it into a large bowl.

Add the soaked bread, onions and garlic, egg, basil, oregano, red pepper flakes, and salt. Mix until all the ingredients are evenly combined.

Roll the mixture into balls about 1½ inches in diameter and set on a large plate or baking sheet.

In a nonstick, ovenproof skillet over medium heat, brown the meatballs in batches of 10, using 2–3 tablespoons of oil per batch. Turn the meatballs until they are a light brown on all sides; this should happen quickly. Turn the heat to low and continue cooking until the meatballs are golden brown all over, about 2–3 minutes. Drain the meatballs on paper towels.

Wipe out the pan, and add 1½ cups of sauce to the pan. Turn the heat to low, add the meatballs, and cook for 8–10 minutes, until they are cooked through.

**To serve:** Preheat the broiler to high. Position a rack in the top third of the oven.

For each serving, place 5 meatballs in a heatproof dish and top with ½ cup of the tomato sauce. Sprinkle with a heaping tablespoon of Parmesan and place under the broiler for 2 minutes, or until the cheese is melted and browned. Sprinkle with chopped parsley and serve.

# John's Playlist:

## Top Ten All-Time Favorite Kitchen Songs and a Dish to Cook to Them

**10. "Swingin'," Tom Petty and the Heartbreakers**—This song gets me going better than a cup of coffee in the morning. Accompanying dish: Perfect BLT with Iberico Bacon (see page 147) with a glass of Bruno Paillard Rosé Champagne.

**9. "Sullivan Street," Counting Crows (live version from MTV's 10 Spot)**—When I'm traveling, lonely, or down, this is what I listen to when I want to be reminded of New York. It lifts me, takes me back, and also allows me to wallow in emotion. Accompanying dish: The Ozersky (see page 137).

**8. "You Shook Me All Night Long," AC/DC**—This is the quintessential preservice, family-meal, rally-the-troops, get-jacked song. Accompanying dish: 44 Farms Meatballs "Parmesan Style" and Spicy Marinara (see page 124).

**7. "Hypnotize," Audioslave**—Powerful and driving, this grunge song just makes me want to get up and work. It's motivational, pushing me to become better every day. Accompanying dish: Octopus with Chorizo, Avocado Relish, and Piquillo Purée (see page 209).

**6. "Egg Man," Beastie Boys**—How can you not love "Sometimes hard boiled sometimes runny / It comes from a chicken not a bunny, dummy"? I skateboarded with these guys when I was younger, so in this song is my own history, the history of New York, and the humble, complex, all-important egg. Accompanying dish: Beef Tartare, Oysters, and Fried Egg (see page 173).

**5. "Wiser Time," The Black Crowes**—I love this band, and this song's slow, driving beat was the soundtrack of my life as I drove down life's highway from the Northeast to Texas. Accompanying dish: Pork Chops and Applesauce (see page 106).

**4. "Times Like These," Foo Fighters (acoustic version)**—This is a very emotional song for me that I've learned note for note on the guitar. All about the art of reinvention, it resonates with every part of my life. It reminds me to stay in the moment. Accompanying dish: The Magic (see page 138).

**3. "Dirt Off Your Shoulder," Jay Z (a cappella version)**—This is stripped-down poetry that's extremely powerful. It's a shoot-from-the-hip song that pounds a potent message. Accompanying dish: Sriracha Pork Belly (see page 149).

**2. "Crazy Mary," Pearl Jam**—This song reminds me of a lot of moments of my life, especially of when I was down on my luck and when I drank too much and people would call me crazy or assume I was losing it. Accompanying dish: Blood Sausage with Uni (see page 206).

**1. "Sympathy for the Devil," The Rolling Stones**—As a lifelong Stones fan, this song has always fascinated and motivated me, and its dark side has always scared me a little bit. Every time I feel myself creeping to the dark side, this song makes me sit up and take notice. Accompanying dish: a hundred-day-aged rib eye steak, cooked in the Back to the Pan method (see page 69).

# BURGERS
# & OTHER SANDWICHES

If this chapter is about anything, it's about integrity. Not the integrity of an individual but the integrity of the sandwich. And make no mistake, the hamburger is a sandwich: the great, all-powerful, American sandwich, but a sandwich nonetheless. Burgers and sandwiches are a big part of the menu at Knife, especially at lunch, and I'm really proud of our creations.

When I talk about integrity in sandwiches, I'm talking about a value that has largely become irrelevant in our current culinary culture. Integrity refers to many facets of the sandwich. Structural integrity—does it maintain its shape as you eat it, or do all the ingredients squirt out the sides? Do the internal ingredients last through every bite, or at the end, are you left with a handful of soggy bread? Textural integrity—do the varying ingredients offer a tapestry of textures, from crunchy to smooth, that make each bite a rousing experience? Integrity of flavor—do the flavors work together, or has the chef tried to pile so much on one sandwich that the result is an indecipherable babble of tastes? And, of course, integrity of ingredients—are you using bread and pungent condiments as a cloak to mask ill-prepared, insipid, mystery meats, or are you treating the sandwich as a way to honor the best ingredients you've got?

Sorry for the rant, but in the rush to use the sandwich as a vehicle for everything, food culture has obliterated a sense of what a good sandwich is. Fast-food culture is the worst offender, where the Double Down from KFC comes to mind (bacon and melted cheese between two fried chicken fillets) as an example of a so-called sandwich completely devoid of integrity. Not just to pick on the lowbrow, the high-priced gourmet burgers created by chefs strike me equally as lacking in integrity too. Putting Wagyu beef, foie gras, black truffles, caviar, blue cheese, and mushrooms between two pieces of butter-soaked brioche is both egregious and a structural mess.

This chapter describes the care we put into our sandwiches. You'll see that there's a precision and a simplicity in each one of them. And if you make sandwiches with simplicity and integrity, the ingredients will have a chance to speak for themselves, and the whole thing will be a pleasure to eat.

# THE
# ART
# OF THE
# BURGER

I'm a fan of classic burgers, of sandwiches you can eat without making a mess, and of a certain simplicity that combines potent flavors and lets them be heard. Sandwiches are built on pushing together contrasting, even clashing flavors. Keep strong flavors simple and clean.

Construction is crucial—just as important as flavor in a sandwich. Sandwiches need to be able to be cut in half (burgers you can, but I think they're better when eaten whole), picked up, and bitten into without tearing. Any sandwich that falls apart is, to me, not successful.

Textures are like flavors—contrast is good. Think about the sensation of biting into a burger. In one smooth motion, your teeth encounter soft-spongy bun, crisp lettuce, pillowy tomato, crunchy pickles and onions, creamy melted cheese, and warm, dense beef. Now that's complexity.

Listed below are all the considerations and techniques that go into a making a superior burger. After that we get into the specific recipes for our acclaimed burgers and other sandwiches.

## THE MEAT

The cost of hamburgers in America is on the rise, and one of the reasons for this, besides a general uptick in the price of beef, is that people are putting short rib and brisket and all sorts of special cuts into their burger meat. That's all well and good, but for me, the integral flavor comes from ground sirloin.

I'm sure most of you will not be grinding your own beef, but I encourage you to do so. You'll be thrilled with the clarity of the flavors and the gracefulness with which it cooks. The best blend for ground beef is 80/20, meat to fat. Trust me, I've done the experimentation. At 70/30, the fat drops out and the patty gets grainy. The ratio of 75/25, meat to fat, works, but 80/20 has better flavor and structure. It's quite simple. Use sirloin beef and straight beef fat. Grind them together at 80/20 and you have the world's best burger meat.

## FORMING THE PATTY

The right amount of meat is 5 ounces. Weigh it out. Too big a patty destabilizes the burger and makes it too meaty. Too small a patty and you only taste condiments, not meat. Five ounces is the perfect amount, right in the middle.

Form the patty in your hands. It's no different from Play-Doh in school. Smash it. Work it pretty hard, but do it quickly, as you don't want fat melting all over your hands. Don't worry about compacting it too much. Use your whole hand: palm and fingers. Make sure that the circumference is clean and smooth, as you don't want end crumbs cooking and falling off. The burger will shrink and buckle when it starts cooking, so the integrity of the patty needs to be solid.

## THE BUN

The bun is of utmost importance! The two crucial aspects are that the bun needs to be durable enough to hold the burger together when you pick it up to eat it, and it has to be something

that's absorbent and spongy, but not so much that it gets soggy and soaked. We use a potato bun that we purchase from a local bakery. Be on the lookout for good buns in your area, and when you find the one, be loyal to that brand.

## HOW TO COOK A BURGER PROPERLY

Let me get this out of the way quickly: Don't cook burgers on the open-fire grill. No matter how iconic the imagery of Dad flipping burgers on the Weber out by the pool, the fact is that burgers both cook and taste much better when seared in a pan. We don't use the grill because the rendering fat inevitably causes flames to leap up and char the burger, giving it a lightly burned exterior and drying out the meat. At the restaurant, we use a plancha or griddle, but at home, use a cast-iron or blue steel pan to perfectly cook a patty without giving up all the juices. Want to cook burgers outside? That's why you have a cassette burner.

Start out with a really hot pan. Rub the patty on both sides with a little softened butter—this isn't for flavoring, but to kick-start the browning process. Then dust one side with kosher salt and freshly ground black pepper.

Add a dash of vegetable oil to the hot pan and let it heat for a few seconds before dumping out the oil—this cleans the pan, lubricates it, and moderates its temperature. Now add a touch more oil and place the burger in the smoking-hot pan, seasoned-side down. Now season the other side with salt and pepper.

It's extremely important to develop a crust on the outside of the burger, which is why we use the pan. The well-browned exterior allows the burger to develop deep flavor and a toothsome texture. Treat the hamburger just like you would a steak. If there's time, don't be afraid to *poêlé* with the liquid fat in the pan (see page 68) to get a little bit of the butter and beef fat back onto the burger.

If you're adding cheese, do it just as the burger has finished cooking. Turn off the burner, layer the cheese on top, and cover the pan to conserve the ambient heat. The cheese will melt as the meat stops cooking.

## CONSTRUCTING THE BURGER

With your lightly toasted or griddled bun, simply place the meat on the bottom bun. We don't butter the bread or add any condiments. That we leave up to the diner. Make sure everything fits neatly—if you're using lettuce or tomatoes, try to not let them extend beyond the span of the bun. Few things look worse than a sloppily built burger.

## OUR STANDOUT BURGER RECIPES

We keep the burger very simple. But we have a couple of options that are meaningful to me on a personal level. These are untouchable, classic burgers that also have soul. Within their construction they contain powerful references to people and times that I won't soon forget. ★

# THE
# OZERSKY

The Ozersky is a loaded burger in more than one way. It's a totem of great happiness and joy, as it was created to the specifications of the late, great food writer and my dear friend Josh Ozersky, who was the most passionate hamburger lover I've ever met. Josh understood the nuances and complexities of the hamburger that most other people take for granted. But there's also a heavy heart, as Josh died suddenly and tragically of natural causes in 2015.

When I first met Josh, we spent eighteen hours in a car driving to Boston, and a lot of that trip was spent talking about hamburgers. After that trip, I was determined to dedicate a burger to Josh. The Ozersky is patterned exactly after what he told me was the most perfect but simple rendering of the hamburger. He liked many kinds of burgers, but this was his Platonic ideal, starting with a 5-ounce patty of great natural beef.

I treat my burgers with the same respect that I treat my steak and cook them on a flat grill or griddle, like the one you'd find at a diner. You can get the same results with a cast iron or blue steel pan. A little butter on the patty gives the burger a nice crust. Josh loved and talked about the creaminess of real American cheese—that much derided orange sheet of hydrogenated vegetable oil and milk solids. And that wisdom can't be denied—if you want to make a burger irresistible, melt American cheese over the top. It adds a soft, creamy textural contrast to the beef. Now what really makes this true to Ozersky's design is that on top we apply two offset squares of American cheese to make a shape reminiscent of a Star of David.

Josh insisted on a nice, squishy potato bun, like Martin's potato rolls. Accept no substitutes. You can order online if they're not available where you live.

SERVES: 1

5 ounces 80/20 ground sirloin
½ teaspoon butter, softened
Kosher salt and freshly ground black pepper
1 teaspoon vegetable oil
2 slices American cheese
Thin slice red onion
1 potato bun, lightly toasted

Pat the ground sirloin into a thin patty, a little bit bigger than the potato bun. Smear butter over one side of the patty and season that side of the patty with salt and pepper. (This is how I always start cooking a burger, by the way.)

In a pan over high heat, heat the oil. Put the burger, seasoned-side down, in the pan and cook until it is brown and crusty, about 4–4½ minutes. While it's sizzling, season the top side of the burger with salt and pepper and baste it with the fat in the pan.

Flip the burger. Lay the cheese slices on top of the burger so they form an eight-pointed star. You can cover the pan at this point to help melt the cheese faster. Cook for another 4–4½ minutes.

Place the onion on the bottom of the bun, top with the burger, cheese-side up, and then the top of the bun.

# THE MAGIC

Named in honor of Magic's Pub on Westhampton Beach, where I first cooked professionally, this is my first memory of a really great restaurant hamburger and the first burger I ever learned how to make.

What made the burger at Magic's, an Irish pub, different is that it came on an English muffin. Practically, it makes a lot of sense. Once the muffin's toasted, the nooks and crannies in the bread catch all the juices from the burger without losing crispness. You may have to toast the English muffin twice to really develop those crunchies.

The muffin-to-burger ratio is also nice, as is the contrast of textures from soft and toothsome to crisply crunchy. As always, give the burger time to develop that crunchy brown crust; it's essential. Crispy bacon is also required. The cheddar is New York sharp, and the bacon adds a little Irish touch. The garnishes for a Magic burger are some soft butter lettuce, a nice thin slice of an in-season tomato, and a thin slice of red onion.

SERVES: 1

5 ounces 80/20 ground sirloin

½ teaspoon butter, softened

Kosher salt and freshly ground black pepper

1 teaspoon vegetable oil

1 English muffin

2 slices applewood-smoked bacon, cooked until crisp

2 slices sharp New York cheddar

1 or 2 leaves butter lettuce

Thin slice vine-ripe tomato

Thin slice red onion

Pat the ground sirloin into a thin patty, a little bit bigger than the English muffin. Smear the butter over one side and season that side of the patty with salt and pepper. In a pan over high heat, heat the oil. When the pan is hot, pour out the excess oil. Put the burger, buttered-side down, in the pan and cook until it is brown and crusty, 4–4½ minutes. Season the top side of the burger with salt and pepper and baste it with the fat in the pan.

Split the English muffin with a fork and toast it until it's golden brown and crisp.

Flip the burger. Place the bacon between the slices of cheddar and put the whole thing on top of the burger. Put a lid on top of the pan to melt the cheese and cook for another 4–4½ minutes.

On the English muffin, layer the lettuce, tomato, and onion. Season with a pinch of salt and pepper. Top with the burger, cheese-side up, cover with the other half of the English muffin, and eat.

# THE BEEF CHEEK BURGER

At the inception of Knife—in my transition from seafood-dominant cuisine to meat—I spent time around a lot of guys who can really only be described as meat fanatics—Josh Ozersky, Daniel Vaughn, the barbecue writer, my friend Mike Hiller. One food that I got into during this period was Mexican barbacoa—deeply braised beef cheek full of unctuous fatty richness. I wanted to replicate that savory richness. At first we tried to cook them sous vide, but the flavor wasn't right. I love braises, particularly for the texture they give meat, so we tried the beef cheek seared, then braised in a classic braising liquid of wine and stock, herbs, and mirepoix, with a little vinegar. The return was mind-blowingly tender, juicy, and flavorful. So then I thought, what are we going to do with it? The answer to that question is always, "If nothing else works, put it in a sandwich." The result was so good, we put it on the menu and never looked back.

SERVES: 4

FOR THE BRAISING LIQUID:

1 tablespoon vegetable oil

1 Spanish onion, diced

2 medium carrots, peeled and diced

6 shallots, ends trimmed and diced

2 cloves garlic

1 small bunch thyme

1 fresh or dried bay leaf

3 cups dry red wine

8 cups veal stock

¼ cup imported red wine vinegar (to be added immediately prior to cooking cheeks)

FOR THE BEEF CHEEKS:

4 (1-pound) beef cheeks, silver skin and cartilage removed

1 teaspoon kosher salt

½ teaspoon freshly ground black pepper

4 tablespoons vegetable oil

4 thick slices crusty bread

Bordelaise sauce (see page 81)

1 cup sautéed sliced cremini mushrooms or truffle shavings, optional

**Make the braising liquid:** Heat the vegetable oil in a large saucepan over medium heat. Add the onion, carrots, shallots, and garlic and cook, stirring occasionally, until the vegetables are soft and caramelized. Add the thyme and bay leaf.

Add the red wine and stir, scraping up all the brown bits of flavor from the bottom of the pan. Cook until the wine has reduced to about 1 cup. Add the veal stock and cook, uncovered, until the mixture has slightly reduced and thickened. Remove from the heat.

(recipe continues)

**Make the beef cheeks:** Preheat the oven to 300 degrees F.

Season the beef cheeks on both sides with the salt and pepper.

In a sauté pan over high heat, heat the oil until almost smoking. Add the beef cheeks and sear on both sides. Transfer the cheeks to a plate.

Add the red wine vinegar to the braising liquid and stir to combine.

Place the cheeks in a roasting pan. Pour the braising liquid over all; the cheeks should be completely covered with the liquid.

Press a piece of parchment paper the size of the roasting pan over the surface of the liquid. Cover the pan tightly with foil. Place the pan on the middle rack of the oven and cook for 3½ hours.

Take the pan from the oven, discard the parchment and foil, and allow the cheeks to cool slightly.

**To serve:** Grill or toast the bread. Warm the bordelaise sauce. Place one cheek on each slice of bread and spoon a generous portion of bordelaise sauce over. Top with the sautéed mushrooms, or if you want to be really extravagant, shaved truffles.

# PATTY MELT

When I was growing up, the patty melt was a staple of the Northeast, an everyday alternative to the hamburger. Our version is basically a grilled cheese sandwich and hamburger mashup with a jalapeño or poblano pepper for contrast. That it's on bread and not a bun makes it more convenient without having to go out to the store to shop for buns. You can't go wrong using Pepperidge Farm white bread in this recipe. The patty technique is the same as with all the burgers. Since I now live in Texas, the addition of poblano or jalapeño adds a little Southwestern spice that I find utterly delicious. Simply blister the peppers in the flame of your gas range or cassette burner (which you hopefully have by now). I like to use pepper Jack cheese for this recipe, but it will work well with whatever cheese you prefer.

SERVES: 1

1 medium poblano or 3 jalapeño peppers
5 ounces 80/20 ground sirloin
2 teaspoons butter, softened
Kosher salt and freshly ground black pepper
1 teaspoon vegetable oil
2 thin slices white bread
4 slices pepper Jack cheese

Roast the pepper(s) over an open flame until the skin blisters. Alternatively, preheat the oven to 425 degrees F. Place the pepper(s) on a baking sheet and roast for 15–18 minutes, turning once or twice so they cook evenly. Cool the pepper(s) and then run them under water briefly. Gently rub off the skin. Cut off the stem end, slit the pepper(s) down the middle, and remove the seeds and stems. Halve the poblano or 1 of the jalapeños. Set aside.

Pat the ground sirloin into a thin patty. Smear ¾ teaspoon of the butter over one side of the patty and season that side of the patty with salt and pepper.

In a pan over high heat, heat the oil. Put the burger, buttered-side down, in the pan and cook until it is brown and crusty, about 4–4½ minutes. Season the top side of the burger with salt and pepper and baste it with the fat in the pan. Flip the burger and cook for another 3–3½ minutes.

Butter one side of each slice of bread with ¼ teaspoon of the butter. In a nonstick skillet over medium heat, melt the remaining 1 teaspoon butter. Place the bread, buttered side down, in the skillet and toast until golden brown.

Place one slice of pepper Jack on each slice of bread. Top each with half the roasted poblano or 1½ roasted jalapeño peppers. Top each side with a slice of the pepper Jack.

Put the burger on one side of the bread, and carefully place the other slice of bread on top, making sure all the sides line up. Press down and flip the burger. Cover and cook for another minute or two to melt the cheese. Put the patty melt on a plate, cut in half straight down the middle, and serve.

# PIMENTO BURGER

What's the difference between a pimento burger and a cheese burger? Besides the peppers, the pimento cheese is much richer than a slice of American cheese. It's spicy, sweet, and creamy all at the same time, my tribute to the South. The leftover cheese makes a great dip and is even better on a grilled cheese sandwich.

SERVES: 4

FOR THE PIMENTO CHEESE:

1 cup mayonnaise

½ teaspoon cayenne

½ teaspoon kosher salt

½ teaspoon freshly ground black pepper

1 cup finely diced roasted red peppers, drained

12 ounces extra-sharp white cheddar, coarsely grated

12 ounces extra-sharp yellow cheddar, coarsely grated

FOR THE BURGERS:

1½ pounds 80/20 ground chuck

2 teaspoons butter, softened

Kosher salt and freshly ground black pepper

2 tablespoons canola oil

4 hamburger buns, split and toasted

4 slices red onion, grilled

4 leaves Bibb or butter lettuce, optional

4 slices tomato

**Make the pimento cheese:** In a large bowl, combine the mayonnaise, cayenne, salt, and black pepper. Whisk until combined.

Add the roasted peppers and cheddars and gently fold into the mayonnaise. Cover the bowl and refrigerate for at least 30 minutes.

**Make the burgers:** Remove the pimento cheese from the refrigerator.

Divide the ground chuck into four equal portions, 6 ounces each. Pat the meat into thin patties, each a little bigger than the bun. Smear ½ teaspoon of butter over one side of each patty and season that side with salt and pepper.

In a pan over high heat, heat the oil. Put the burgers, buttered-side down, in the pan and cook until they are brown and crusty, 4–4½ minutes. Season the top sides of the burgers with salt and pepper and baste them with the fat in the pan. Flip the burgers and cook for another 3 minutes. Put a dollop of cheese on top of each burger. Cover the pan and cook for a minute, until the cheese is melted and gooey.

Place a bun on each of four plates and stack with the onion, lettuce, and tomato. Top each bun with a burger, cheese-side up, and cover with the other half of bun.

## PROTOTYPE SANDWICHES, PERFECTED

The sandwiches that follow aren't flashy. They're not over the top. They're simply meant to be the ideal versions of some classic sandwiches. Of course, making them with integrity is key. Don't overstuff them or unbalance them. Remember that part of the pleasure of a great sandwich is not having it fall apart on you. ★

# PERFECT BLT WITH IBERICO BACON

This recipe brings back memories of childhood. A BLT is the simplest thing I can imagine and one of the first things I really loved. In the summer, my mother grew the most incredible tomatoes, and we always had fresh lettuce from a local farm stand. And—sorry, gourmets—I'm an eternal devotee to soft, squishy white bread, which just has the perfect texture for sandwiches.

In form, this is a classic BLT. The way I've elevated the sandwich is to use Iberico or *pata negra* ham from Spain. It's the überbacon, made from an Iberian breed that has a black coat and black hooves, thus *pata negra*. Available at good gourmet grocers online, it's more expensive than standard bacon, but well worth the cost for its rich, nutty flavor. It's really like eating ham candy.

In the summer, we have amazing heirloom or vine-ripened tomatoes. But what if you want a BLT in the winter? Tomatoes might be plump and red looking in the store, but they won't taste like they do in summer. The solution is to slowly roast the tomatoes in the oven with salt and pepper and a little olive oil to concentrate the flavors and bring out the sweetness. It really works and provides the sweetness of summer year round.

Because of my insistence on perfectly constructed sandwiches, I love the flavor and texture of Bibb lettuce, which has broad, tender, delicate leaves that still have some structure.

Finally, it's not a BLT unless it has mayonnaise. I can make twenty different versions of flavored mayonnaise at home, but for me the perfect BLT needs Hellmann's. Certain things in life cannot be replaced or improved upon. Hellmann's mayonnaise is one. (The other? Heinz ketchup.)

(recipe continues)

3–5 slices Iberico bacon

½ teaspoon butter

2 thin slices commercial white bread, like Pepperidge Farm

1½ teaspoons mayonnaise

2 leaves Bibb or Boston lettuce, hard vein removed

3 thin slices ripe tomato, or slow-roasted tomato

In a nonstick skillet over medium heat, place the Iberico bacon. Cook for 2 minutes and then turn the heat to low and continue to cook, turning the bacon occasionally so it cooks evenly. The bacon should be crisp but still tender.

Pour out the rendered fat, leaving about 1 teaspoon in the pan.

Spread ¼ teaspoon of the butter on one side of each slice of bread. Place the bread, buttered-side down, in the pan and toast until golden brown. Flip and continue cooking for another minute. Remove the bread.

Spread ¾ teaspoon of the mayonnaise on each side of the sandwich. Top each side with a leaf of lettuce. Top one side with the tomatoes and then the bacon. Close the sandwich.

Gently press down on the sandwich and cut on the diagonal.

# ROASTED TOMATOES

This is more a technique than a recipe.

Preheat the oven to 250 degrees F. Line a rimmed baking sheet or sheet pan with parchment paper. Slice as many tomatoes as you want about ½ inch thick, and lay the slices in a single layer in the pan. Drizzle generously with extra-virgin olive oil, and sprinkle less generously with kosher salt, freshly ground black pepper, and fresh thyme leaves. Roast for 2–3 hours, checking after 2 hours, until the tomatoes are wrinkled and caramelized but not completely dried out. Store in the refrigerator for up to a week.

# SRIRACHA PORK BELLY SANDWICH

The recipe for the sriracha pork belly in this sandwich comes from my friend Josh Smith. His use of the pork belly is virtuosic, and he's inspired me to take it as seriously as he does. The savory spice of sriracha just matches so beautifully with the sweet unctuousness of the pork belly. You can find hoisin sauce in the Asian section of most well-stocked supermarkets, Asian markets, or on the Internet. I use sweet Corsicana pickles from Texas, but any bread-and-butter chip will do.

SERVES: 1

1 tablespoon canola oil

½ teaspoon butter

Steamed bun (see recipe page 150)

3 slices (about 3 ounces total) sriracha pork belly (see page 189)

⅛ teaspoon kosher salt

⅛ teaspoon freshly ground black pepper

1 tablespoon hoisin sauce

Sriracha, for garnish

Scallion oil (see page 150), for garnish

3–4 slices sweet pickles, for garnish

Cilantro leaves, for garnish

In a nonstick pan over medium-high heat, warm the canola oil. Spread butter over one side of the bun, and put it buttered-side down in the pan. Cook until golden brown, a little darker than a hamburger bun, almost burned. Cook the other side until the same golden brown color. Set it aside on a paper towel.

Season the pork belly with the salt and pepper. Wipe out the pan and raise the heat to high. Place the pork belly in the pan and immediately turn the heat down to medium. You want to warm the meat and get it a little crispy and caramelized, like bacon, and render some of the fat. Flip the pork belly and cook the other side.

Take ½ tablespoon of the hoisin sauce and make a small circle in the middle of a dinner plate. Place the bun on top of the circle of hoisin. Spread the top of the bun with the remaining ½ tablespoon hoisin. Place the warm pork belly on the bun.

Make 5 or 6 dots of sriracha around the edges of the plate. With a spoon, drizzle the scallion oil over the plate.

Top the pork belly with the pickle slices and garnish with a sprig of cilantro.

(recipe continues)

## SCALLION OIL

**1 bunch scallions, roots trimmed and dark
  green parts removed**

**¼ cup 75/25 canola/olive oil blend
  (see page 88)**

Coarsely chop the scallions. Place the scallions
and oil in a blender and blend on high until you
have a smooth purée.

Use immediately or store.

## STEAMED BUNS

If you have leftover buns, they can be
refrigerated in an airtight container for 3–4 days.

YIELD: 12 BUNS

**1 tablespoon plus 1 teaspoon dry yeast**

**1½ cups warm water**

**4½ cups bread flour, plus additional for dusting**

**3 ounces sugar**

**3 tablespoons instant nonfat dry milk powder**

**1 tablespoon kosher salt**

**½ teaspoon baking soda**

**½ teaspoon baking powder**

**⅓ cup bacon fat or vegetable shortening**

**1 tablespoon vegetable oil**

In the bowl of a stand mixer fitted with the
dough hook, combine the yeast and water.
Add the bread flour, sugar, milk powder, salt,
baking soda, baking powder, and bacon fat or
shortening. Turn the mixer on low and mix until
the ingredients form a ball.

Oil a large bowl and turn the dough into the
bowl. Cover and put in a warm, draft-free place
until the dough doubles in size, about an hour.

Turn the dough onto a floured surface and
roll out (it doesn't matter what shape) to
½ inch thick. Let the dough rest, covered, for
30 minutes.

Preheat the oven to 300 degrees F. Bring a kettle
of water to a boil.

Using a 3½- or 4-inch round cookie or biscuit
cutter, cut circles from the dough.

In a rimmed baking sheet, place a wire rack big
enough to fit inside the pan. Lightly oil the rack.
Pour enough hot water into the pan to come just
below the rack.

Place the buns in a single layer on the rack and
cover the pan with foil. Carefully place the pan
in the oven and steam for 3–4 minutes.

# JT'S GRILLED CHEESE

Who doesn't love a grilled cheese sandwich? Like most people, I've worshiped this American staple since I was a kid. And I still love it today. A good grilled cheese should be both decadent and simple. My version was inspired by the beautiful grilled cheese made at Hog Island Oyster Company in San Francisco's Ferry Building. It's big and gooey and irresistible.

As I've said before, when it comes to bread, do as you like, but I still like the commercial white bread I grew up with. Pay attention to the construction and uniformity by layering the goat cheese in between the two cheddars. The combination of two cheddars with an herbed goat cheese provides a sophistication that's joyfully undermined by the hedonistic sponginess of the white bread.

SERVES: 4

1 cup fresh soft goat cheese, like Montrachet

1 tablespoon chopped chives

1 heaping tablespoon thinly sliced basil leaves

1 tablespoon very thinly sliced scallion, white and light green parts

Pinch kosher salt

Pinch freshly ground black pepper

3 tablespoons plus 2 teaspoons butter, softened

8 slices commercial white bread, like Pepperidge Farm

16 thin (⅛-inch-thick) slices sharp New York cheddar

16 thin (⅛-inch-thick) slices white Vermont cheddar

Preheat the oven to 350 degrees F.

Place the goat cheese in a small bowl. Add the chives, basil, scallion, salt, and pepper and work it all into the goat cheese using a fork or your very clean hand until everything is incorporated. Divide the cheese mixture into four equal portions and set aside.

In a nonstick skillet over medium heat, melt 1½ teaspoons of the butter. Butter one side of 2 slices of bread, using about ½ teaspoon per side. Place the bread, buttered-side down, into the pan. Place 2 slices of the New York cheddar on each slice of the bread, then 2 slices of the Vermont cheddar. Turn down the flame so the bread doesn't burn before the cheese melts. Take one portion of the goat cheese mixture and press it evenly over one side of the bread and top with the other slice of bread.

Place the skillet in the oven for 4–5 minutes, until the cheese is soft and melted. Cut on the diagonal and serve.

Repeat with the remaining bread and cheeses to make 3 additional sandwiches.

# REUBEN

All New Yorkers have logged time at Katz's Delicatessen, which is still churning out amazing Jewish deli food on Houston Street. And in the annals of deli sandwiches, the Reuben has to rank near the top, if not at number one. You need a really good Jewish rye bread with caraway seeds for this. Some old-school bakeries, like Orwasher's in New York and Zingerman's in Ann Arbor, Michigan, still make it. Sometimes called corned rye, it's dusted with cornmeal and has a great sour rye smell. If you don't have a good Jewish bakery near you or don't want to order online, go with Levy's; that's what we use at Knife. At Knife, we make our own pastrami (you'll find a recipe on page 186) and sauerkraut, but if you're not that ambitious, use the best-quality fresh deli pastrami you can find. If you can't get fresh sauerkraut from a deli or farmers' market, bagged or jarred will work. I'd avoid the canned stuff.

It may be traditional to put Thousand Island or russian dressing on the Reuben, but to me that's sacrilegious. It's a much better sandwich without all that sweetness—a liberal spread of mustard goes much better with the briny, pickled flavors of the meat and kraut. You can melt the cheese on the stove top, but I love the way finishing it in the oven preserves the integrity of the sandwich while just softening the cheese.

SERVES: 1

⅓ cup sauerkraut

5 ounces thin-sliced lean pastrami

2 slices New York–style rye bread

2¼ teaspoons butter, softened

½ teaspoon Dijon mustard

4 thin slices jarlsberg cheese

Kosher dill pickle, sliced in half lengthwise, for garnish

Preheat the oven to 350 degrees F.

In a small saucepan over medium-low heat, warm the sauerkraut in some of its brine.

In a nonstick skillet over medium heat, warm the pastrami. You want a little of the fat to melt, but you don't want to cook or crisp it. Remove the pastrami from the pan.

Spread one side of each slice of rye bread with ¾ teaspoon of the butter. Melt the remaining ¾ teaspoon butter in the pan. Place the bread, buttered-side down, in the pan.

Spread ¼ teaspoon of the Dijon mustard over one side of each slice of the bread.

Put 2 slices of jarlsberg over one side of each slice of the bread. Pile the pastrami on one side of the bread.

Drain the sauerkraut and pile it on the pastrami. Top with the other slice of bread and press down gently. Place the pan in the oven for 4 minutes, or until the cheese has melted.

Remove the pan from the oven, place the sandwich on a plate, and cut the sandwich in half straight across. Put the pickle halves on the plate and serve.

# CUBAN

As a New Yorker, I did as many New Yorkers do when they need to get away—traveled to Miami a fair bit. That's where I was introduced to this sandwich long before it became a national hit. Knife is known for beef, but we also revere the pig here, and this sandwich is one of our many homages. It uses two forms of pork: sriracha pork belly, a recipe developed by meat genius and great friend Josh Smith of Boston; and Benton's country ham from Tennessee.

Smash the avocado with a fork to make it more pliable and easier to spread on the sandwich—but don't make guacamole! If you have a panini machine, by all means assemble the sandwich and press it in that. If not, do it in a frying pan on the stove, and press the top of the sandwich firmly with a plate or another small frying pan. Finishing in the oven completes the crisping and binds the ingredients together. The consistency of this sandwich—of all of my sandwiches—is very important. It shouldn't messily spill out onto the plate, and every bite should taste uniformly of ham, bread, mustard, cheese, avocado, and pickle.

Use a good country ham, like Benton's. Deli ham is okay, but a good country ham gives the sandwich an extra layer of rich, salty flavor. You want a soft—not a crusty—roll for this. A hero roll is perfect. And if you don't want to make the sriracha pork belly or don't like heat, just use plain roasted pork belly (see page 185).

SERVES: 1

3 (½-inch thick) slices sriracha pork belly (see page 189)

3 ounces thin-sliced country ham, like Benton's

1½ teaspoons unsalted butter

1 soft roll, sliced in half

½ avocado

½ teaspoon Dijon mustard, or more to taste

4 thin slices, about 1 ounce, good imported Swiss cheese, like Gruyère

5–6 kosher dill pickle slices

Preheat the oven to 350 degrees F.

Lay the pork belly slices in a nonstick skillet over medium heat. Cook it like you would bacon, about 3 minutes on a side until the fat renders and the slices are brown and caramelized, but not crisp. Set the pork belly aside on a plate and wipe out the pan.

Place the pan back over the heat and add the ham and cook for about 2 minutes, just until it's warmed through and the fat starts to render out. Put the ham on the plate with the pork belly.

Turn the heat to medium low. Melt ½ teaspoon of the butter in the pan.

Spread both the inside and outside of the roll with the remaining 1 teaspoon butter, about ¼ teaspoon of butter per side. Place the roll in the pan, cut-side down, and toast until it's a nice golden brown. If there's extra butter in the pan, pour it out.

(recipe continues)

Scoop the flesh of the avocado into a small bowl and roughly mash it with a fork. You want some chunks and texture.

Flip the bread in the pan and spread the mustard evenly over the cut sides. If you like more, add more.

Place 2 slices of cheese on each half of the roll. On one half of the roll, layer the pork belly, pickle slices, and ham. Spread the mashed avocado on the other side and place that half on top of the other half of the sandwich.

Using a sandwich plate or your very clean hand, press down on the top of the sandwich to compress it; don't press so hard that the ingredients come out the side. (If they do, trim them away.) Weight the sandwich with a small skillet and place the whole thing in the preheated oven. Bake for 2 minutes and then flip the sandwich, replace the small skillet, and cook for another 2 minutes.

Place the sandwich on a plate, slice on the diagonal, and serve.

## CONDIMENTS

I don't keep a lot of condiments around, but for me, the two I've included here (along with a good Dijon mustard) are the kings of condiments—delicious and useful in multiple situations. Once you make them, you'll find yourself reaching for them for so many things you cook. And they'll keep really well in the kitchen. ★

# CHIPOTLE MAYO

This is the simplest recipe in the book, but it's a great condiment for all the fried foods and will add complexity to almost any sandwich. Chipotle peppers are nothing more than smoked jalapeños; they're Bobby Flay's favorite ingredient and very Texan. We find them canned in adobo sauce. To them, we add Hellmann's mayonnaise, one of nature's perfect foods. Green Tabasco is made with jalapeños and is slightly milder than traditional Tabasco sauce.

You could add ¼ cup chopped cilantro leaves, but that makes it another sauce. I wouldn't, but do as you wish. The chipotle mayo will keep in the refrigerator for at least a couple of weeks, and it's not just delicious with avocado fries. Try it with french fries, grilled shrimp, even steak.

YIELD: 2½ CUPS

1 (7-ounce) can chipotles in adobo
2 cups Hellmann's mayonnaise
1 tablespoon fresh lime juice
1 teaspoon green Tabasco

Put the chipotles in adobo and mayonnaise in the jar of a blender. Purée for a minute, until the chipotle peppers are completely broken down and the mixture is smooth and a rich red clay color. Add the lime juice and green Tabasco and pulse briefly.

# BACON JAM

This was created to go with our bacon tasting—yes, bacon strips with bacon jam—but I think its beautiful, chunky, sweet, tart flavor can be a great condiment for almost anything. You can spread it on toast, dab it on a sandwich or burger, fry it with eggs.

We use Nueske's applewood-smoked bacon, and we cook slowly to render for about 10 minutes until the bacon sort of melts but doesn't color. Make sure not to add the garlic to the hot bacon fat, as you don't want it to brown and crisp. Cook it slow and low until the liquid has evaporated and it has the consistency of preserves or jam. A final few pulses in the food processor creates the ultimate smooth but slightly chunky texture.

Oh, and as for the ketchup in this, I use Heinz.

YIELD: 2–3 CUPS

**1 pound applewood-smoked bacon, diced**

**1½ cups diced Spanish onion**

**4½ teaspoons finely chopped garlic**

**¼ cup red wine vinegar**

**½ cup maple syrup**

**½ cup ketchup**

**½ teaspoon cayenne**

**¼ teaspoon ground nutmeg**

**¼ teaspoon ground cinnamon**

**¼ cup bourbon**

In a saucepan over medium heat, cook the bacon. The bacon should start to soften but not color at about 10 minutes.

When the fat in the bottom of the pan begins to boil, add the onion, stir to combine, and let the onion-bacon mixture cook for another 8–10 minutes, until the onions become translucent and soft.

Add the garlic and cook for 1–2 minutes. Add the vinegar and stir well, scraping up any brown bits from the bottom of the pan. Add the maple syrup, ketchup, cayenne, nutmeg, and cinnamon. Stir to combine, and after 15 minutes, add the bourbon. Turn the heat to low and simmer for 45 minutes, or until the mixture has thickened and is the consistency of a preserve or jam.

Line a rimmed baking sheet with parchment paper. Spoon the jam onto the baking sheet and refrigerate until cool, about an hour.

Spoon the jam into a food processor fitted with the steel blade, and pulse until the mixture has a homogeneous texture and the fat emulsifies into the jam. Scrape down the sides of the bowl occasionally.

# CHARCUTERIE & TARTARES

If the answer to the question of what to do when life gives you lemons is "Make lemonade," the answer to the question of what to do when life gives you a pile of meat trimmings is "Make tartare and charcuterie." I've been making these things for decades, and they continue to give me great pleasure as reminders of how a little ingenuity and touch can produce a dish that far exceeds the potential of humble ingredients.

Good meat can be delicious in any number of ways besides the conventional cooking methods we use most of the time. Raw meat, as you see in a dish like tartare and carpaccio, emphasizes delicacy and texture over the rich flavors that develop with cooking. Tartare is also a great vehicle for the other savory notes used in the seasoning—mustard, pickles, capers. The same is true no matter what protein you use, as you'll see with the lamb and tuna tartare recipes in this chapter.

Charcuterie shows us yet another side of meat, where it's partially cooked through a process of curing or brining. These processes happen in a cool temperature and use salt and/or sugar to preserve the meat, producing rich, tangy, savory flavors that can't be achieved with other methods.

While tartares and charcuterie were originally thrifty ways to use trimmings and other parts that were tougher sells, today they can be delicacies in their own right. So that means, feel free to use higher-end cuts to up the quality of your dishes. For instance, we throw trimmings (from great cuts) into tartare, but we also use some high-end meat like the filet and the sirloin. And a quick note on safety: If you're buying fresh, good-quality beef and grinding it yourself, there should be no issues with eating or preparing raw beef. Just keep it cold when making it, and if there's a delay between preparation and eating it, keep it in the fridge.

## TARTARE

I love tartare in any shape and form. It's a lean, clean, and satisfying merger of the mellow taste of raw protein with a series of enlivening condiments. It's great with wine or beer and never taxes the palate, which is why it makes such a fantastic appetizer, though it can also work as a mellow main course. At Knife, we always offer several tartares. The meat is ground to order, and it's all mixed by hand to achieve the perfect texture.

One of the most decadent things you can do with tartare is serve it alongside something cooked, a combination I find irresistible. I first encountered it in Paris in 1995 at Alain Ducasse's now defunct Spoon, Food & Wine. They served a hanger steak with a mound of steak tartare piled on it—it was one of the best dishes of my life. The tartare was liberally laced on top of the dish, providing an eye-opening contrast between this vinegary, marinated hanger and the lushness of the tartare. ★

Ground-to-Order Steak Tartare in the Style of 21

# GROUND-TO-ORDER STEAK TARTARE IN THE STYLE OF 21

When I was a kid, every Christmas my father would take us to the 21 Club in New York City. They made the most incredible tartare I ever had and did it tableside with great flair. The flavor, aroma, and texture always stayed with me, so I came up with this version, re-created from my childhood memories.

I suggest using great beef in the following ratio: 25 percent sirloin (for its fat) and 75 percent filet mignon, which is leaner, for its tenderness. Hand-cut tartare is popular these days, but I prefer the silky texture that comes from putting it through a grinder. You can grind the beef yourself, if you have a hand grinder or a grinder attachment for your stand mixer, or you can ask your butcher to grind it for you. It should be ground twice, using the coarse plate.

I use two stainless steel bowls when making this. The lower one is filled with ice, and the top one, in which I mix the tartare, rests on the ice to keep cold so the fat doesn't start to melt out of the beef. For the capers, use the smallest size—called nonpareil. Take the time to drain them and chop them by hand; food processors just turn them into a paste. Likewise chop the cornichons by hand.

At the 21 Club, tartare was served in a big loaf for the entire table, and the waiter would break an egg on top of it. We instead serve it individually in 4-ounce portions, firmly packed into a ring mold. To place the egg yolk, once the ring mold is removed, make an indentation in the center of the tartare and then remove the top of the quail egg's shell and release the egg into your hand. Let the white slide through your fingers while retaining the yolk to place in the center of the tartare. If you don't have quail eggs, use the yolk of a small hen egg, but serve it with 8 ounces of tartare. Naan, an Indian flatbread, is available in most well-stocked supermarkets.

SERVES: 4

- 12 ounces filet mignon, double ground using the coarse plate
- 4 ounces well-marbled sirloin, double ground using the coarse plate
- 1 teaspoon kosher salt
- ½ teaspoon freshly ground black pepper, plus additional for garnish
- 1 tablespoon Dijon mustard
- 1 tablespoon finely chopped nonpareil capers
- 1 tablespoon chopped cornichons
- 3 tablespoons thinly sliced scallion
- 2 tablespoons grated Parmesan cheese
- 3 tablespoons plus 1 teaspoon extra-virgin olive oil
- 4 quail's or small hen's eggs
- Pinch Maldon sea salt, for garnish
- Whole cornichons, for garnish, optional
- Toasted naan bread, for serving

Place the ground beef in a stainless steel bowl. Nest the bowl in a larger bowl filled with ice. This will keep the fat from getting too soft and mushy.

Add the salt, pepper, mustard, capers, cornichons, scallion, Parmesan, and 3 tablespoons of the olive oil. Mix well until everything is completely combined and you have a homogeneous mixture.

One portion is a quarter of the meat mixture. You can use an ice cream scoop or spoon to mound the tartare on individual plates, or use a ring mold to create a uniform shape.

Make an indentation in the center of each portion.

Crack an egg, carefully separate the white from the yolk, and slip the yolk in the indentation. Repeat with each portion. Reserve the whites for another purpose.

Sprinkle each portion with a pinch of Maldon sea salt and garnish with additional cornichons, if desired. Drizzle the tartare with ¼ teaspoon of the olive oil, and grind some black pepper around the plate. Serve with toasted naan.

# BIGEYE TUNA TARTARE WITH SCALLION, SRIRACHA, CUCUMBER & WASABI TOBIKO

Tuna tartare is one of the most abused, overused, predictable, leftover '80s dishes ever to appear in restaurants. But I love it. It's clean, healthy, and satisfying. And if you make it right, it doesn't have to be dull or bland.

We use the best tuna we can find and try to make it as fresh and clear and transparent as possible. For this Asian-style tuna tartare, try to buy tuna from a larger fish, as older, bigger tuna will have developed the flavor, fat, and depth smaller ones lack. Tuna tartare cannot be ground; it has to be hand sliced. Using a sharp knife, slice it into strips, going across the grain. If there's any white muscle fiber or tissue, gently remove it with your hands. Then further cut the fish into a small to medium dice. I look at tuna tartare as each bite being a little bit of sashimi. It's different from our look at beef tartare, which we grind.

White soy sauce is a very delicate, clean, less saline version from Japan brewed with more wheat and unaged compared to a typical, dark soy. If you don't have white soy sauce, just omit it, as dark soy will be too strong. Simmering cucumbers in rice wine vinegar for a brief moment gives a quick, delicious pickle and provides a great top for the tartare and a platform for the wasabi tobiko. You can simply make a neat pile of the tartare on the plate or use a ring mold, as we do at the restaurant.

SERVES: 4

½ cup unseasoned rice wine vinegar

12 thin slices english or other seedless cucumber

1 pound high-quality fresh ahi, yellowfin, or bigeye tuna steak, cut about 1 inch thick

¾ teaspoon kosher salt

½ teaspoon freshly ground black pepper

Zest of 1 medium lime

2 tablespoons thinly sliced scallion, white and light green parts

1 tablespoon plus 1 teaspoon wasabi tobiko

1 teaspoon sriracha

1 tablespoon white soy sauce

3 dashes green Tabasco

3 tablespoons plus 4 teaspoons extra-virgin olive oil, preferably Ligurian

(recipe continues)

In a small nonreactive saucepan over medium heat, bring the vinegar to a simmer. Add the cucumber slices and remove the pan from the heat and let cool completely. The slices will be lightly pickled and translucent.

With a very sharp knife, slice the tuna across the grain into strips, as you would a flank steak. If there are any white fibers or tissue, pull them off and discard them. Cut each strip lengthwise down the middle and then crosswise into medium-size cubes.

Place the tuna in a bowl and nest the bowl in a larger bowl filled with ice. Season with ¼ teaspoon of the salt and ¼ teaspoon of the black pepper. Toss gently to combine. Add the lime zest, scallions, 1 tablespoon of the tobiko, the sriracha, white soy sauce, and green Tabasco and mix well. Add 3 tablespoons of the olive oil and mix. Taste, and add up to ½ teaspoon salt and ¼ teaspoon pepper more. (I like it spicy. You may not.)

Divide the tuna mixture evenly among four plates. Top with each portion with 4 slices of the pickled cucumber and ¼ teaspoon of tobiko. Sprinkle a teaspoon of olive oil around the tuna on each plate.

# BEEF TARTARE, OYSTERS & FRIED EGG

This tartare preparation came about because one day—I must have been missing Paris in the wintertime—I had the hankering for both steak tartare and some oysters. It occurred to me that I was craving a form of surf and turf, so I created this simple dish, and we put it on the brunch menu. Use your favorite oysters; they're all delicious. Your fish market can open them for you if you don't have the skills; just make sure they don't discard the oyster liquor. When you add an egg, tartare becomes an instant brunch item. Add the oyster and its juice to the top of the tartare for some briny complexity.

SERVES: 4

**1 recipe steak tartare (see page 168)**
**4 teaspoons butter**
**4 eggs**
**12 oysters, opened**
**Maldon sea salt, for garnish**
**Extra-virgin olive oil, for garnish**
**Freshly ground black pepper, for garnish**

Plate the beef tartare.

Melt the butter in a nonstick skillet over medium heat. Break the eggs into the skillet and cook sunny-side up.

Put 3 oysters on top of each portion of tartare, and pour the oyster liquor over the oysters and the tartare. Top each portion with an egg and season the egg with a pinch of Maldon salt, a drizzle of extra-virgin olive oil, and a grind of black pepper.

# LAMB TARTARE

Most people don't think of eating lamb raw. So when I was looking for another variation, a new perspective on the genre of tartare, it was natural to go to the lamb. I was simply exploring the frontiers of tartare and trying to be a little different.

In lamb tartare, we use the less expensive shoulder cut, as opposed to leg, rack, loin, and so on. Shoulder has more fat, like 80/20 ground beef, which is what you need here. As usual, I prefer domestic lamb, as it has great flavor without being too gamy. You can grind the shoulder yourself, if you have a hand grinder or a grinder attachment for your stand mixer, or you can ask your butcher to grind it for you. Ask for it to be ground twice, using the coarse blade.

This recipe starts similarly to the beef tartare but takes its own turn with a somewhat Greek accent thanks to the addition of feta cheese (instead of Parmesan in the beef), jalapeños, and fresh mint. The addition of scrambled egg makes this dish brunch-worthy, but I love it any time of day.

If you have any left over, the jalapeño/mint oil will keep, covered, in the refrigerator for 2–3 days. Drizzle it over tacos or grilled fish.

SERVES: 4

2 jalapeño peppers, cored and seeded

½ cup packed mint leaves, plus torn leaves for garnish

½ cup 75/25 canola/olive oil blend (see page 88)

1 pound lamb shoulder, double ground using the coarse plate

1 teaspoon kosher salt, plus additional to taste

½ teaspoon freshly ground black pepper, plus additional to taste

3 tablespoons thinly sliced scallion, white and light green parts

2 teaspoons Dijon mustard

2 tablespoons plus 4 teaspoons shredded or finely crumbled Greek feta cheese

2 tablespoons butter

4 eggs

2 teaspoons chopped chives, plus more for garnish

1 teaspoon finely shredded mint

Place the jalapeños, mint leaves, and oil in a blender. Starting on low and increasing the speed to high, blend for 30 seconds. Set aside.

Place the lamb in a stainless steel bowl. Nest the bowl in a larger bowl filled with ice. Add the salt, pepper, scallion, mustard, and 2 tablespoons of the feta. Add ⅓ cup of the jalapeño/mint oil and mix well with a metal spoon until everything is completely combined. If there are any chunks of feta, break them up with the mixing spoon and continue mixing until you have a homogeneous mixture. Taste and add more salt and pepper if necessary.

In a nonstick skillet over medium-high heat, melt the butter. Break the eggs into a small bowl and whip them with a fork. Pour the eggs into the pan and stir. Add the chives and shredded mint. Cook until the eggs are softly scrambled. (That's my preference; if you like them firmer, that's okay too.)

One portion is a quarter of the meat mixture. You can use an ice cream scoop or spoon to mound the tartare on individual plates, or use a ring mold to create a uniform shape. Surround each portion with an equal portion of the scrambled eggs; you want each person to get a bit of the egg and lamb in every bite.

Sprinkle 1 teaspoon of feta over each plate. Drizzle some of the jalapeño/mint oil over the tartare. Scatter some torn mint leaves over the plate; sprinkle with some chopped chives.

# CHARCUTERIE

My first trip to France did not begin auspiciously. On day one, I was laid up in our hotel near the Jardin du Luxembourg with the flu, and culinary school was beginning only two days later. I was freaking out. I was just starting to recover when I had to drag myself out of bed and to the school for the audition, during which I cut my finger pretty badly. Things were not going my way, not to mention the challenges I was experiencing as a first-time American in Paris who didn't speak a lick of French.

And then things turned around. I recovered from the flu. I was admitted to the school's highest level. And then I was at a newsstand buying an English-language paper to look through apartment classifieds when the woman next to me started up a conversation. She was American and inquired about my situation. I told her I was going to La Varenne and was desperate to find an apartment. "What a coincidence," she said. She had a little artist's loft above her own place, perfect for a young couple. We got lucky: The top-floor garret was beautiful, an amazing place to live in Paris. The second stroke of luck was that on the ground floor of the building was a charcuterie shop, the first I'd ever seen. It was filled with all sorts of incredible items—salami, pâtés, rillettes, terrines. Over time, I got to know the gentleman who ran it. He showed me everything: how he added bread to meat to make pâté, how he ground the meat and fitted it into casings. I fell in love with his craft.

A lot of charcuterie—salami and long-cured ham, for instance—is hard to master and takes time, space, and climate control. However, there are a few things easy enough for even the dabbler to perfect. Making them gives loads of satisfaction. You should learn how to make a mousse or a terrine or rillettes. It just requires a little time and attention. Here are a couple of delicious and ridiculously easy charcuterie staples to make at home—and one terrine recipe, the headcheese, which is more difficult to render, but a stunner when you pull it off. ★

# CHICKEN LIVER MOUSSE WITH PORT WINE GELÉE

Chicken liver mousse used to be found at every bistro in France, and this is the perfect version I learned in my youth. If you don't have (or like) port, use another sweet dessert wine, like cream sherry, to make the gelée. I serve this in individual 6-ounce Mason jars, but any similar-sized dishes will do, as long as the gelée covers the entire surface.

SERVES: 4

FOR THE CHICKEN LIVER MOUSSE:

1 pound chicken livers

2 tablespoons butter, plus ½ cup melted butter

2 tablespoons minced shallot or scallion

⅓ cup cognac

¼ cup heavy cream

½ teaspoon kosher salt, plus more to taste

⅛ teaspoon ground allspice

⅛ teaspoon freshly ground black pepper, plus more to taste

FOR THE PORT WINE GELÉE:

1 cup port

¾ teaspoon (about half a packet) unflavored gelatin

**Make the chicken liver mousse:** Carefully examine the livers and cut away any green or black spots. Cut the livers into ½-inch pieces.

In a skillet over medium-high heat, melt the 2 tablespoons butter. Add the shallot and the liver, and sauté for 2–3 minutes, until the livers are firm but still rosy inside.

Scrape the contents of the skillet into the jar of a blender.

Pour the cognac into the skillet and raise the heat to high. Boil the cognac, scraping up any bits from the bottom of the pan, until it has reduced to 3 tablespoons. Pour it into the blender jar.

Add the cream, salt, allspice, and pepper to the jar. Cover and blend on high speed until the mixture becomes a smooth paste. Add the ½ cup melted butter and blend until completely incorporated and you have a uniform mixture.

Use the back of a spoon to force the mixture through a sieve into a bowl; discard any lumps left behind. Taste and add more salt and pepper if necessary.

Pack the mousse into four 6-ounce Mason jars and cover with wax paper. Refrigerate for 2–3 hours, until the mousse has set.

**Make the port wine gelée:** In a small nonreactive saucepan over medium-low heat, warm the port to about 175 degrees F; do not let it boil. Add the gelatin and stir until it dissolves completely. Remove the pan from the heat and pour through a fine-mesh strainer into a heatproof measuring pitcher. Set aside to cool to room temperature; it will thicken slightly.

Remove the mousse from the refrigerator, uncover, and top each portion with 1 tablespoon of the thickened gelée, spreading it so it covers the entire surface of the mousse. Refrigerate, covered, until the gelée sets, about 1 hour.

# BASIC PORK RILLETTES

Rillettes, a delicious mash of slow-cooked meat and fat, is your gateway drug to charcuterie addiction. It's the simplest method of curing and preparation, and everyone loves it. What more can you ask of a dish?

When it comes to this kind of dish, you have full poetic license, as long as you follow the basic instructions. The adventure and excitement of doing these simpler recipes is that you can play with spices and seasonings, textures, and flavors. It's an open book. Once you've made the pork, you can go on to other types of rillettes as you choose. I've seen salmon and trout rillettes, duck and boar. You can make rillettes from almost anything, but pork is the ultimate. If you don't have pork stock in your freezer, you can use chicken stock. Homemade is best, but the store-bought kind will do. You can find rendered pork fat, or lard, online, at Mexican markets, or at farmers' markets. If you have any left over after making the rillettes, it will keep almost indefinitely, covered, in the refrigerator. Serve it as a snack on a crust of bread dabbed with Dijon mustard and a glass of wine.

YIELD: 1 (9 X 5-INCH) LOAF

2 cups dry white wine

4 sprigs thyme

2 dried bay leaves

4 shallots, ends trimmed, sliced

3 cloves garlic

1 bone-in pork shoulder, 3–4 pounds

1 teaspoon kosher salt

½ teaspoon freshly ground black pepper

3 tablespoons canola oil

3 quarts pork stock

3 quarts rendered pork fat, warmed until liquid

3 árbol chiles

In a deep container large enough to hold the pork shoulder, combine the wine, thyme, bay leaves, shallots, and garlic. Add the pork shoulder, cover, and refrigerate overnight.

Preheat the oven to 250 degrees F.

Remove the pork from the marinade and pat it dry; reserve the marinade. Season the pork with the salt and pepper.

In a skillet over high heat, sear the pork in the canola oil on all sides until golden brown.

Place the pork in a deep roasting pan and pour in the marinade, pork stock, pork fat, and chiles.

Put the pan in the oven and cook for 3 hours. Carefully flip the pork over, return it to the oven, and cook for another 3 hours or until falling-apart tender.

Remove the pan from the oven and let the pork cool in the liquid until it's room temperature. Remove the pork from the pan to a plate and carefully strain the liquid into a large bowl. Skim off as much of the fat as possible, and reserve.

In a large saucepan over medium-high heat, cook the liquid until it has reduced by half and is thick enough to coat the back of a spoon.

Take the pork meat off the bone and place it in the bowl of a stand mixer fitted with the paddle attachment. Turn the mixer on high and slowly add the reserved cooking liquid. When the pork is shredded and most of the liquid absorbed, slowly add half the reserved fat.

Line a 9 × 5-inch loaf pan with plastic wrap so the ends of the wrap hang over the edges of the pan. Pack the pork mixture into the loaf pan, cover, and refrigerate overnight.

To serve, remove the pan from the refrigerator, invert onto a serving plate, and remove the plastic wrap.

Slice and serve at room temperature.

# NEAL'S HEAD— CHEESE TERRINE

Neal Liston is my in-house butcher. He cuts up the meat, supervises the aging room, and occasionally makes a dish. This headcheese has been a work in progress. I've seen him through many evolutions of this, but this is the version that hit all the marks. It's unique. Traditional headcheese comes from the pig, but we found that the beef version is lighter, creamier, and just as tasty. It has that dense, rich consistency of tongue. All it requires is a cow's head, which we boil, and we pick all the meat off the skull— everything but the eyes and the brain—and use the natural juices and gelatin in the broth to set the terrine.

By the way, this is an incredible terrine, but it's not something that I expect a home cook to tackle. It requires a huge cauldron and a huge burner to boil it, and it makes an enormous quantity. That said, if any of you have access to a commercial kitchen and are ambitious, this is a wonderful appetizer and should be served with cornichons and a grainy mustard.

SERVES: 25

1 whole cow head

2 medium yellow onions, diced

4 stalks celery, diced

2 carrots, peeled and diced

1 jalapeño, stemmed, seeded, and ribs removed, diced

1 bunch thyme

2 fresh or dried bay leaves

5 shallots, diced

¾ cup packed chopped cilantro leaves

1 bunch chives, minced

4 tablespoons unseasoned rice wine vinegar

5 tablespoons kosher salt

1 tablespoon freshly ground black pepper

Place the cow's head in a pot large enough to hold it and cover the head with water. It should be fully submerged. Add the onions, celery, carrots, jalapeño, thyme, and bay leaves.

Bring the water to a simmer (this will take a while, but don't let it boil) and cook for 5 hours, or until the meat on the head is tender. Test by pulling off a piece of the meat; it should come away easily.

Remove the head to a bowl or rimmed plate and let cool to room temperature. Add any liquid that accumulates back to the pot.

Strain the liquid and discard the solids. You should have about 8 quarts.

Return the liquid to the pot and boil until it has reduced to one-tenth the volume, about 3 cups.

(recipe continues)

When the head is cooled, pick the meat from the bone, shred it, and reserve in a large bowl.

Remove the tongue from the head and peel off the membrane. Discard the bones and the membrane. Dice the tongue and add to the reserved head meat.

Mix 1¼ cups of the reduced liquid into the tongue and head meat. Add the shallots, cilantro, and chives and stir to mix well.

Add ½ cup of the liquid, the vinegar, salt, and pepper. Mix well and discard the rest of the liquid.

Pour the mixture into a 9 × 5-inch loaf pan, cover with plastic wrap, and refrigerate until firm, at least 24 hours.

When you're ready to serve, turn the headcheese out of the pan onto a cutting board, and with a very sharp knife, cut into 1-inch-thick slices.

# BRINES AND CURES

In recent years, both chefs and diners have come to a better understanding of the deep synergies of the ancient art of preservation. Not only does preservation allow a meat protein to be stored for later consumption, the process also magically imbues the meat with more complex and alluring flavors. We see this in everything from beef jerky to salami to bacon.

For a long time I didn't believe in brining. I just didn't think that it did anything. But then the pork belly craze hit, and I gave brining a new look. I'd never cooked pork belly before, and the first few times I tried cooking it, it came out bland and fatty. At some point I saw a video of Gordon Ramsay cooking a pork belly that he had brined, and it started to make sense. (See? Even I learn from TV chefs!) Shortly after, a friend made this 30-day brined pork belly, and it was the sweetest, most gelatinous, incredible stuff. My view shifted.

These forms of preservation all start with some degree of salting, either a "wet cure" in the form of a brine or a "dry cure," which is just a dusting of salt and spices and sometimes sugar. We use both techniques at Knife, less for preservation than for the wonderful, complex flavors with which they imbue the meats. Here are a number of brined and cured appetizers. ★

# BRINED PORK BELLY

Pork belly is the part of the pig that becomes bacon when it's salted and cured, but it makes a great roast too. Brining is a great way to get some herbal flavor complexity into a rich, unctuous belly of pork while the sugar and salt in the brine also firm up the belly's texture without sacrificing tenderness. This method takes a few days because of the brining, but the amount of work for this is small, and the payoff is big—delicious, flavorful, rich pork belly that can be served as is or in a variety of other ways.

You can make the brine ahead of time, but it cannot be reused. The pork needs to sit in the brine for at least 3 days and up to 10 days, so plan ahead! I think 7 days is the sweet spot.

SERVES: 6

FOR BRINING THE PORK BELLY:

1 piece pork belly, 3–4 pounds

2 quarts warm water

2 big sprigs thyme

3 dried bay leaves

½ cup sugar

½ cup kosher salt

6 cloves garlic, stem ends removed

FOR ROASTING THE PORK BELLY:

1 tablespoon kosher salt

1½ teaspoons freshly ground white pepper

Warm water to cover the bottom of the roasting pan

2 cloves garlic, halved lengthwise

2 big sprigs thyme

1 tablespoon extra-virgin olive oil

**Brine the pork:** Cut the pork in two pieces. In a container big enough to hold the pork and water, add the thyme, bay leaves, sugar, and salt to the water and stir until the sugar and salt dissolve.

Gently crush the garlic with the flat of a knife and add it to the brine. Submerge the pork in the brine, cover, and refrigerate for at least 3 days and up to 10 days.

**Roast the pork:** When you're ready to cook the pork, preheat the oven to 400 degrees F. Remove the pork from the brine and rinse it. Discard the brine. Season the pork with the salt and white pepper.

Pour warm water into a roasting pan fitted with a rack. You want to cover the bottom of the pan, but the water should not touch the pork. Put the garlic and thyme on the rack and lay the pork, fat-side up, on the rack. Drizzle the pork with the olive oil. Cover the pan with foil and roast for 2¾–3 hours. Remove the foil from the pan and carefully pour off the fat that has accumulated in the pan.

Remove the pork belly from the oven and let the roast rest for 10 minutes before slicing and serving.

If you're using this in another recipe, let the pork rest until it reaches room temperature. Put a pan the same size or larger (like a half sheet pan) on top of the roast and weight it evenly with cans or a heavy skillet. Let the pork rest overnight in the refrigerator and cut into blocks or slices, and proceed with the recipe.

# KNIFE
# PASTRAMI

Brisket may be the favorite meat of the Texas barbecue world, but long before that, it was a popular cut in Eastern Europe to turn into what we now call pastrami. One of the tougher cuts of meat, a whole brisket has two ends, a thin, lean end and a rounded, fatty end. The thinner end makes a leaner pastrami, the fat end a meaty, lush, New York Jewish deli–style pastrami. Many butchers sell just the lean end, but if you like a fattier and more marbled piece of brisket, ask them to include the fatty end. When prepping the brisket, trim the excess fat, leaving a thin layer on top, which mostly renders during cooking.

The pink salt called for in this recipe is known as curing salt, which just means it is a mixture of table salt and sodium nitrite. Sodium nitrite, which prevents the growth of bacteria and botulism, is dyed pink to prevent its confusion with normal salt. You can buy it at a specialty cooking store or on the Internet. Pickling spice is a mixture of whole spices, which may include mustard seed, allspice, coriander, cloves, ginger, bay leaf, and cinnamon. After a 7–10 day brining process, the brisket has technically become corned beef. Smoke is what turns it into pastrami. Slathering the brisket with mustard both seasons the meat and helps the rub of black pepper and coriander stick to the meat. No additional salt is needed, thanks to what's in the brine and the mustard.

If you have a smoker or barbecue, smoke the brisket for 45 minutes per pound at 225 degrees F. If you don't have a smoker, just cook it in an oven at 250 degrees F without smoke. It won't exactly be pastrami, but it will be delicious.

SERVES: 8–10

FOR BRINING THE BRISKET:

**1 piece well-marbled beef brisket (butt end), 4–5 pounds**

**2 quarts warm water**

**1 tablespoon plus 1½ teaspoons pink curing salt**

**½ cup sugar**

**¾ cup kosher salt**

**2¼ teaspoons pickling spice**

**2 large cloves garlic, halved**

**¼ cup honey**

FOR PREPARING THE PASTRAMI:

**1½ cups Dijon mustard**

**1 cup finely ground black pepper**

**1 cup finely ground coriander**

**Brine the brisket:** Trim some of the external fat from the brisket. You want to get rid of the excess, but leave enough to baste the meat and keep it moist.

In a large nonreactive container, pour the warm water. Add the pink curing salt, sugar, kosher salt, pickling spice, garlic, and honey. Stir until the honey has completely dissolved.

Put the brisket into a container big enough to hold the meat and the brine; the brisket should be completely submerged. Place a piece of parchment paper or plastic wrap over the brisket and weight it with a large plate or platter.

(recipe continues)

Refrigerate the brisket for 7–10 days. When you take the brisket out at this point, you have corned beef. Now we're going to turn it into pastrami.

**Roast the brisket:** Place the meat on a flat surface and pat dry. Coat the meat on both sides with the mustard, using all the mustard. Really slather it on.

In a bowl, combine the pepper and coriander. Lightly pack the mixture first on the top, then the bottom of both halves of the meat. Try not to leave handprints. The surface should be completely coated.

Preheat the oven to 250 degrees F. Place the brisket on a rack in a roasting pan. Cover the pan with foil and cook for 45 minutes per pound, about 3–4 hours. About 20 minutes before the end of the cooking time, take the foil off the pan and turn up the heat to 400 degrees F.

# SRIRACHA PORK BELLY IN THE STYLE OF PEKING DUCK

The recipe for this scintillating sriracha pork comes from my friend Josh Smith, the meat wizard of New England charcuterie. It's fantastic as an app or as party food to prep ahead of time and offer as passed hors d'oeuvres at a gathering or reception.

YIELD: 3–3½ POUNDS PORK BELLY

2 tablespoons kosher salt

2 tablespoons turbinado sugar

1 cup sriracha

¾ teaspoon finely grated lime zest

½ cup fish sauce

3–4 pounds fresh pork belly

In a bowl, combine the salt, sugar, sriracha, lime zest, and fish sauce.

Place the pork belly in a nonreactive container, pour the mixture over, and rub it in. Cover and refrigerate the pork belly for 36–72 hours. Remove the pork belly from the marinade and cut it in half. Place each piece of the pork belly into a ziplock plastic bag, squeeze out all the air, and seal the bag.

Fill a pot or container large enough to hold both bags of pork belly three-quarters full of warm water. Attach a sous vide circulator, plug it in, and set it to 140 degrees F. Immerse the pork belly and cook for 18–24 hours.

Use immediately in a sriracha pork belly sandwich (page 149), or store for up to 2 weeks in the refrigerator. Try it instead of bacon for breakfast or on a BLT.

# SALADS, STARTERS & SIDES

Well, maybe it's not a surprise that everything exclusively non-meat-related in this book has been relegated to the back pages. But that organizational detail doesn't reflect at all on the importance of the dishes in this chapter. I love these starters, salads, and sides, and I think they're absolutely crucial to a good meal.

I want first courses that are both memorable and distinct from the meat courses that follow. The idea is that you have an incredible meal that *happens* to end with the best steak of your life. Therefore, I put a lot of thought into the rest of the menu, which has led me to a slate of dishes that range from the classic to the exotic. I like to focus particularly on the quality of umami, the so-called fifth taste, which we know as a sense of savory or meaty deliciousness.

Respect for vegetables has long been a theme in my life. Farm to table is now a culinary cliché, but going back to my youth on Long Island, that's how we'd often get our produce—from a farm stand not far from our house. I thought nothing of it at the time, but we were often eating locally and seasonally—today's buzzwords of contemporary American cuisine. You'll see this in the vegetable side dishes here and the salads. To this day, I think of salads as being an essential part of pretty much every meal, so I offer here recipes for simple, basic salads that never fail to make a crisp and perky foil to all the dishes in the book.

As for starters, I want them to be exciting. Being a proud French-trained chef, I tried to imbue these dishes with what I didn't see in steakhouses: a special touch that says there's a chef in the kitchen and not just a team of cooks. So I went for dishes that had some character and flair. That's why below you'll find a section of exotic takes on the steakhouse cliché of surf and turf, such as bone marrow and caviar or uni and blood sausages.

## SALADS

When I was a kid, all I ate was steak and lamb chops. I would make myself iceberg salad with tomatoes and vinaigrette. So early on, like muscle memory, I fell in love with the contrast between salad and steak. To this day, I can't really eat a steak without seeing it accompanied by a fresh, bright green salad. Here are the recipes for some of my longtime favorites. ★

# CLASSIC GREEN SALAD WITH ITALIAN DRESSING

During World War II, my mother hung out in a community of Italian women while my father was away serving in the military. They taught her how to cook their way, which then became our way. This was her standard Italian dressing, which I had practically every day growing up, and is still near and dear to my heart. This is a classic green salad, simple and elegant. The beautiful lettuces are different colors and textures, and the carrots and radishes add crunch. It can be served family-style or on individual plates.

You needn't use an expensive extra-virgin olive oil for this dressing, as the flavor would be lost. If you like a hint of that olive oil pepperiness, I suggest just adding a tablespoon, while making the rest with a neutral oil like canola oil. This can easily be made and kept in a jar and stored for weeks. Just shake the jar vigorously to emulsify the dressing before serving. It will separate again over time, but it's easy enough just to shake it back into a mixture.

SERVES: 4

(recipe continues)

FOR THE VINAIGRETTE:

4 cloves garlic, peeled and stem ends removed

⅓ cup packed fresh basil leaves

⅛ teaspoon finely ground black pepper

¼ teaspoon kosher salt

1 cup 75/25 canola/olive oil blend (see page 88)

1 generous tablespoon of extra-virgin olive oil

½ cup red wine vinegar

FOR THE GREEN SALAD:

1 small head lola rosa lettuce

1 medium head Bibb or Boston lettuce

1 small head red-leaf lettuce

1 small head green-leaf lettuce, or ½ small head frisée

5 small heirloom or baby carrots, peeled

⅓ cup packed thinly sliced french breakfast radishes (about 4 radishes)

4 large basil leaves, thinly sliced, or 1 tablespoon small whole leaves

1 tablespoon fresh dill fronds

1 tablespoon Italian parsley, thinly sliced

4 7-minute hard-boiled eggs

Pinch coarse sea salt or kosher salt

Cracked fresh black pepper

**Make the vinaigrette:** Lightly crush the garlic and place it in a nonreactive bowl. Add the basil leaves, pepper, salt, oils, and vinegar. Whisk the vinaigrette until it emulsifies and set aside.

**Make the salad:** Wash and dry the lettuce. Remove the large outer leaves of the lola rosa, Bibb or Boston lettuce, and red-leaf lettuce and set them aside for another purpose. You want to use the hearts of the lettuces.

Trim off the stem ends of the lola rosa, Bibb or Boston lettuce, red-leaf lettuce, and the green-leaf lettuce or frisée. Separate the leaves of the lettuces and place them in a large salad bowl.

Use a vegetable peeler to make ribbons of carrots; you want ⅓ packed cup. Add the carrot ribbons to the bowl. Add the sliced radishes, basil, dill, and parsley.

Add 3 tablespoons of vinaigrette (leaving behind the garlic cloves and basil leaves) to the bowl and toss the salad with your impeccably clean hands or tongs. Place the salad on a platter or individual plates.

Peel and halve the hard-boiled eggs and season the yolks with a pinch of sea or kosher salt; garnish the salad with 2 egg halves.

Grind a couple of turns of black pepper over the salad and serve.

# PERFECT VINAIGRETTE

A crisp green salad with a great French vinaigrette is the perfect racy foil to a steak. This is what I consider to be the perfect vinaigrette, more classically French than Italian. The ingredients in this are all strong on their own, but actually soften each other when combined. The vinegar and mustard act on the shallot, tempering its raw fire and leaving it sweet and mellow. Finishing with a drop of lemon juice gives it that little bump of acidity to really take it over the top. Add this to any salad mixture you like: The herb-laden green salad on page 193 is perfect with this vinaigrette too.

YIELD: 2½ CUPS

1 heaping tablespoon minced shallot

1 heaping tablespoon Dijon mustard

½ cup imported red wine vinegar or champagne vinegar

2½ cups 75/25 canola/olive oil blend (see page 88)

1 teaspoon kosher salt

½ teaspoon finely ground black pepper

Squeeze of fresh lemon juice

In a nonreactive bowl, whisk together the shallot, mustard, and vinegar. Set the bowl aside for a minute or two to allow the vinegar and mustard to break down the shallot and make it sweeter.

Drizzle 1 cup of the oil down the side of the bowl, whisking constantly until the dressing is creamy and emulsified. Taste the dressing; if it is too tart, whisk in up to another 1½ cups of oil.

Whisk in the salt and pepper and a squeeze of lemon juice.

# MY CAESAR

Caesar salad would be a cliché these days if it were not just so delicious. In this world of hypergarlicky and pungently anchovied dressing, however, I like to go back to the classic incarnation of the salad, when it was a more elegant emulsion. I follow the directions of Cardini, the gentleman who invented the salad in Tijuana in 1924. The surprising fact that no one remembers about this original version of the salad is that it doesn't contain actual anchovies. Instead, it uses Worcestershire sauce, which is made from anchovies and provides the umami kick.

Mine differs from Cardini's in that I've adapted it to be made in a food processor for convenience and consistency. I'm also using whole garlic cloves instead of the garlic-infused olive oil that Cardini called for. Also, I use raw egg yolks instead of a coddled egg. Source the freshest eggs you can, but raw eggs shouldn't be eaten by the very young, the very old, pregnant women, or anyone with a compromised immune system.

The salad is truly best when made with the light green interior heart of the romaine. Don't throw the outer leaves away—just save them for a different salad mix. If you don't have time to make your own croutons, buy some focaccia, which is already laden with olive oil, and cut it up into cubes and toast it in the oven for a couple of minutes. This dressing recipe is enough for 7–10 people, but if you have leftover dressing, it will keep in your refrigerator for at least a week.

SERVES: 2 AS AN ENTRÉE (WITH ADDITIONAL MEAT, SHRIMP, OR FISH) OR 4 AS AN APPETIZER

**FOR THE CAESAR DRESSING:**

**3 egg yolks**

**6 medium garlic cloves, peeled and stem ends removed**

**1 tablespoon Worcestershire sauce**

**⅛ teaspoon Tabasco**

**¼ teaspoon Dijon mustard**

**¼ cup plus 2–3 tablespoons fresh lemon juice**

**1½ teaspoons red wine vinegar**

**½ teaspoon freshly cracked black pepper**

**½ cup packed grated Parmesan cheese, plus additional for garnish**

**2 cups 75/25 canola/olive oil blend (see page 88)**

**¼ cup extra-virgin olive oil**

**FOR THE SALAD:**

**2 hearts of romaine, any dark leaves removed and tops and ends trimmed**

**¼ teaspoon freshly cracked black pepper**

**1 tablespoon grated Parmesan cheese**

**FOR THE CROUTONS:**

**2 slices good white bread**

**2 tablespoons clarified butter**

**Kosher salt and freshly cracked black pepper**

**Chunk of Parmesan or Pecorino Romano cheese**

**Make the dressing:** In the bowl of a food processor, place the egg yolks and garlic. Process until the garlic is finely chopped, about 1 minute. Shut off the processor and add the Worcestershire sauce, Tabasco, mustard, ¼ cup of the lemon juice, the vinegar, pepper, and Parmesan. Process until completely blended. While the machine is running, add the blended oi and then the olive oil in a thin stream. Don't be shy; the dressing won't break. You should have a nice creamy dressing that just coats the back of a metal spoon. Taste and add the remaining 2–3 tablespoons lemon juice to the dressing, a tablespoon at a time, until you're happy with the consistency and taste.

**Make the salad:** Cut the romaine hearts crosswise into 1–1½ inch pieces. Place the pieces in a large bowl and add the pepper and Parmesan. Add 5 tablespoons of the dressing and toss until the lettuce is coated. Divide the salad between 2 serving plates (or 4 plates, if serving as an appetizer).

**Make the croutons:** Cut the crusts off the bread and cut the bread into 1-inch squares. Place the clarified butter into a skillet or sauté pan over high heat. Throw in one square of bread; it should toast but not burn. Once the sacrificial crouton is golden brown, remove it and throw the rest of the bread into the pan. Season with a pinch each of salt and pepper. Gently stir and toss the croutons until toasted and golden on all sides.

**To serve:** Divide the croutons between the salads. Using a cheese plane or a vegetable peeler, shave thin strips of Parmesan over the salads and garnish with grated Parmesan. Serve immediately, while the croutons are still warm.

# WEDGE SALAD

The wedge. It can be as simple or as complicated as you like. I take the middle road with tangy, irresistible Roquefort dressing. The blue cheese dressing starts with an emulsified red wine vinaigrette, which then gets thickened and expanded with sour cream and mayonnaise. The blue cheese augments the creaminess and provides that funky blue flavor counterpoint to the vinaigrette base. If you want to be decadent, you can add 4–5 ounces of real Roquefort cheese, which is more complex and intense than basic blue cheese from the store. And, no, there's no bacon on this salad. I'm a purist! Make the dressing and tomato garnish at least 4 hours and up to a day ahead.

SERVES: 8

FOR THE BLUE CHEESE DRESSING:

½ large shallot

½ teaspoon chopped garlic

1½ teaspoons Dijon mustard

¼ cup imported red wine vinegar

1 cup 75/25 canola/olive oil blend (see page 88)

1 cup Hellmann's mayonnaise

½ cup sour cream

2 cups crumbled mild blue cheese

½ teaspoon freshly ground black pepper

½ teaspoon kosher salt

2 tablespoons fresh lemon juice

½ cup crumbled Roquefort cheese, optional

FOR THE TOMATO GARNISH:

10 cherry or grape tomatoes, halved, mixed colors if available

Pinch kosher salt

Pinch freshly ground black pepper

2 teaspoons finely minced chives

½ teaspoon finely minced shallot

½ teaspoon fresh lemon juice

1 tablespoon extra-virgin olive oil

FOR THE SALAD:

2 large heads iceberg lettuce, cored, damaged leaves removed, and cut into 4 wedges each

½ cup crumbled blue cheese or Roquefort

**Make the dressing:** Put the shallot, garlic, mustard, and vinegar in the jar of a blender. Start on low and gradually increase the speed to high and blend for 35 seconds. Slowly add the oil, ½ cup at a time, and blend until the dressing is completely emulsified.

Pour the dressing into a bowl and whisk in the mayonnaise and sour cream. Add the blue cheese and whisk until combined. Add the pepper, salt, and lemon juice and whisk.

Add ½ cup of the Roquefort, if using, and whisk to combine. Cover the bowl and refrigerate for at least 4 hours or up to 1 day.

**Make the garnish:** In a nonreactive bowl, gently toss the tomatoes with the salt, pepper, chives, shallot, lemon juice, and olive oil. Cover and refrigerate for at least 4 hours or up to 1 day.

**Make the salad:** Place each wedge of iceberg lettuce on a plate. Distribute the tomatoes evenly around the wedges. Pour 3–4 serving spoonfuls of dressing over each wedge and garnish with a tablespoon of crumbled blue cheese, or Roquefort if you used it in the salad dressing.

## STARTERS

For the starters section of the Knife menu, we have some over-the-top meaty options like a bacon tasting. But one thing I wanted to do with this genre was to play with the concept of surf and turf, that well-worn steakhouse cliché. When we were designing the original menu, I said to the team, "We're not putting surf and turf on this menu. It's heavy and weird to pair lobster tail and filet mignon, not to mention it's often used as gimmick to pry a hundred dollars from a customer." Instead, I repurposed this concept into a series of dishes far more exotic and exciting.

At Knife, we use the idiom of surf and turf to explore the visceral, powerful flavors of the earth and the sea. On paper, these flavor combinations seem bizarre, but in practice, they really work. This is mostly because they highlight the sensation of umami through combinations of some of the world's richest and most flavorful substances like sea urchin and blood, caviar and marrow, octopus and chorizo. These dishes are unusual but also simple to make (especially if you buy the blood sausage at a butcher shop) and will wow your guests at a dinner party. ★

Bacon-Crusted Bone Marrow with
Celery Hearts and Tesar's Caviar

# BLOOD
# SAUSAGE
# WITH UNI

I love what Chris Ying wrote about blood sausage in the food magazine *Lucky Peach*, calling it "the purest distillation of sausage philosophy: Take the least obviously usable part of the animal—the blood—and make something delicious." He notes the versions produced by various countries: black pudding (UK), boudin noir (France), morcilla (Spain), and so on. If you don't want to make your own—which is an ambitious production for a home chef—any store-bought blood sausage of the above varieties will work for this combination.

I was making blood sausage one day and noticed that we had some beautifully fresh uni in the kitchen. When it's good, there's nothing else like uni (sea urchin)—I love its intense umami, lush texture, and perfect portrait of the sweet, briny ocean. We'd been using the urchin on the bone marrow, but when I tasted it against the iron-rich, spicy intensity of the blood sausage, I instantly made a switch and used the uni on this dish. It worked like a charm, creating a fascinating contrast—creamy, briny uni against meaty, chewy blood sausage.

If you do choose to attempt making blood sausage, you can order pork blood from your butcher or an Asian market. Likewise, either pork or lamb sausage casing can be ordered from your butcher; I prefer lamb for its texture and subtler taste. If your casings come in a solution, they need to be rinsed before use. If you get them packed in salt, you need to soak them in cold water for an hour, changing the water once or twice. A stand mixer with a sausage-stuffing attachment helps with this recipe.

SERVES: 4

1 pint pork blood

1 tablespoon oat flour

2 tablespoons red wine vinegar

3 ounces cured pork lardo, diced

1 medium yellow onion, diced

1 clove garlic, minced

3 leeks, ends trimmed and well washed, diced

½ teaspoon cayenne

2 tablespoons kosher salt

1 fresh pork casing

75/25 canola/olive oil blend, for sautéing (see page 88)

Extra-virgin olive oil, for garnish

Maldon sea salt, for garnish

12 pieces of uni, for garnish

Place the pork blood, oat flour, and vinegar in a blender. Starting on the lowest setting and increasing the speed to high, blend until the mixture is perfectly smooth.

In a skillet over medium heat, cook the lardo until the fat is melted. Add the onion, garlic, and leeks and sauté until the vegetables are soft and translucent. Remove the pan from the heat and let cool to room temperature.

In a large bowl, combine the pork blood mixture, sautéed vegetables, cayenne, and salt.

Attach the sausage casing to a funnel and tie the other end shut. Slowly force the sausage mixture into the funnel, being careful not to break the sausage casing. When the casing is full, tie off the end.

Bring a pot of water large enough to hold the sausage to 160 degrees F. Place the sausage in the water and weight it down with a clean kitchen towel. Gently poach the sausage for 20–30 minutes, until firm. Do not let the water boil.

Gently remove the sausage from the water and place it on a plate lined with a paper towel. Cover with plastic wrap and refrigerate for at least 12 hours, until it is completely cool and firm.

When you are ready to serve, remove the sausage from the refrigerator and carefully slice it with a very sharp or serrated knife into 1½-inch-thick slices.

In a nonstick skillet over high heat, sear the sausage pieces in a little oil on all sides until the cut surface is crisp; flip and cook the other side until the sausage is warmed through.

Put three slices of sausage on each plate. Drizzle a little olive oil over the slices and sprinkle with Maldon salt. Top with 1 piece of uni for every 2 rounds of sausage and serve.

# BACON-CRUSTED BONE MARROW
## WITH CELERY HEARTS & TESAR'S CAVIAR

After taking the uni away from the bone marrow, the question was what to put with the marrow. I wanted decadence and a contrastingly pungent flavor to mild, fatty marrow and thought of my friendship with the Passmore Ranch family, which produces caviar from their farm-raised sturgeon in Sacramento. Every year I go out to Sacramento and blend my own version with my old friend Matt Accarrino of San Francisco's SPQR. We biopsy the sturgeon, remove the ovary and egg sack, and harvest the roe. We each decide on our own salt content and flavor profile. Find a brand of caviar that you enjoy with enough salty tang to play against the creamy bone marrow, smoky bacon, and crunchy-bitter celery.

Marrow bones are the femur bones of cows. Ask your butcher to cut the bones into 6-inch lengths and then cut them in half lengthwise to expose the marrow. The marrow has to be soaked overnight; plan accordingly. The bones can be reused over and over again; simply wash, boil, and dry them after use, or run them through the dishwasher. They can be stored in a covered container at room temperature.

This is a very rich dish. At the restaurant, we serve 2 halves per person as a starter, but you might want to share or serve 1 bone half per person. If you have leftover bread crumb mixture, you can store it in the freezer indefinitely. I started using rock salt for plating this dish when a guest ate a spoonful from the mound of kosher salt on which the bones were resting.

SERVES: 4, 2 SIDES PER SERVING

8 (6-inch) halves of center-cut marrow bone, 10–12 ounces

10 ounces applewood-smoked bacon, cut into small dice

8 slices thin-sliced white sandwich bread, like Pepperidge Farm, crusts removed (feed the crusts to the birds)

2 tablespoons parsley leaves

2 teaspoons kosher salt

2 teaspoons freshly ground black pepper

Rock or kosher salt, for plating

40 celery heart leaves, for garnish

2 teaspoons extra-virgin olive oil, for garnish

Maldon sea salt, for garnish

Whatever kind of caviar you prefer, as much as your budget will allow

Fill a bowl with ice water. Remove the marrow from the bones with a spoon. If there are veins in the marrow, remove them and discard. Place the marrow in the water. Cover and refrigerate overnight. This will get rid of any blood or impurities and firm up the marrow.

Scrape the bones clean with a spoon. Place them in a pot of boiling water and boil for 5–10 minutes. Remove the bones, drain, pat dry, and reserve.

Place a skillet over high heat. When it is hot, add the bacon and cook until crisp and golden. Don't let it burn; you don't want any brown bits in the bottom of the pan. Let the bacon cool for 3–4 minutes.

Drain the marrow and pat it dry. Place the marrow in the bowl of a food processor and add 3 tablespoons of the bacon bits. Pulse to combine. Start the food processor and slowly add 3 tablespoons of the bacon fat. Process until you have a smooth mousselike mixture; it will have the consistency of peanut butter. Once you have a smooth, uniform texture, stop the machine immediately. Scrape the mixture into a container and refrigerate until it is firm, at least 1 hour and up to 3 weeks.

Wash and dry the bowl of the food processor. Place the bread in the food processor and pulse for 30 seconds, until you have nice coarse crumbs. Add the parsley leaves, salt, and pepper and pulse until the parsley is incorporated. Add the rest of the bacon and its fat and process, stopping the machine to scrape down the sides of the container occasionally. You want a

uniform, moist mixture. Transfer the mixture to a container and set aside.

When ready to serve, remove the bone marrow mousse from the refrigerator and let it come to room temperature; you want it to have the consistency of a stick of butter.

Preheat the broiler to high and position the rack in the upper third of the oven.

Spoon the bone marrow mousse into the bone cavity; overfill it just a little. Smooth the top of the mousse with an offset spatula so it is even with the bone, pack down the ends, and clean any excess mousse from the bone.

Sprinkle bread crumbs over the surface of the mousse, covering it completely. Gently pat down the crumbs.

Fill a baking pan large enough to hold the bones in a single layer with rock or kosher salt and moisten the salt to form a bed for the bones. Place the bones on the salt and broil until the bread crumbs are lightly toasted, 3–4 minutes. Check the bones after 90 seconds to make sure they're not browning too quickly. Some of the marrow will run; that's okay.

To serve, on each plate build a pile of rock or kosher salt. Nest the bones (or bone) in the salt. In a small bowl, toss the celery leaves with the olive oil. Garnish each serving with 3–5 celery leaves and a sprinkle of Maldon sea salt. Garnish with as much caviar as your taste and budget allow.

# OCTOPUS
## WITH CHORIZO, AVOCADO RELISH & PIQUILLO PURÉE

This recipe might seem like an oddity in a beef book, but it's one of my signatures here at Knife and a great appetizer to provide contrast to the beef that follows. Plus, I just love octopus. In New York in the late 1990s, I started encountering it on a lot of menus. I fell in love with its lush creaminess, but I didn't know how to cook it, and whenever I tried, it came out tough and flavorless. So I went out and dined, and I talked to octopus suppliers. I chatted with chefs about how they cooked it.

The art of cooking octopus is to find ways to make it tender. Many, many different ways exist. I've heard of people pounding it with a ninety-pound hydraulic jack and also, as is traditional in Japanese cooking, tenderizing it with a massage. The Greeks pound it on rocks and dry it in the sun. Some people freeze it and then thaw it.

Going on *Top Chef*, I was so afraid they were going to surprise me with octopus and that I might embarrass myself on television that I practiced and practiced with it until I came up with this method to get wonderfully tender octopus in a time short enough for television. The solution? A pressure cooker. The 18 minutes of pressure cooking at 15 psi is equivalent to about a 3-hour braise, and it comes out tender, but firm enough to not fall apart. (I never ended up having to do this on the show.)

Lastly, I wanted to offer some notes on a couple of the ingredients: Xanthan gum is a plant-based food additive. Often used in gluten-free baked goods to help bind them (in place of the gluten found in flour), it's also found in commercial foods like salad dressing and is used to keep ingredients from separating. You can probably find it in the gluten-free section of your grocery store or on the web. Black garlic is just garlic aged to an extreme degree and undergoing a sort of fermentation that not only turns it black, but gives it an exotic and complex flavor, melding a molasses-like sweetness with a mellow, garlicky funk, minus the allium's characteristic heat. More and more, you can find it in various forms—cloves, pastes, and powders—at gourmet grocers, some Whole Foods, and even online (try blackgarliccity.com).

SERVES: 4

(recipe continues)

FOR THE PIQUILLO PURÉE:

11 medium piquillo peppers, drained

1 tablespoon seasoned rice wine vinegar

¼ cup extra-virgin olive oil

⅛ teaspoon kosher salt

⅛ teaspoon freshly ground white pepper

1 teaspoon xanthan gum

FOR THE AVOCADO RELISH:

1 Hass avocado, pitted, peeled, and diced

2 piquillo peppers, drained and patted dry, diced

4 cloves black garlic, peeled and diced

¼ teaspoon kosher salt

¼ teaspoon freshly ground black pepper

2 tablespoons extra-virgin olive oil

2 teaspoons fresh lemon juice

4 basil leaves, sliced into thin ribbons

FOR THE CHORIZO:

8 ounces Spanish chorizo, skin removed

2 teaspoons extra-virgin olive oil

FOR THE OCTOPUS:

8 octopus tentacles, chilled (see headnote)

Kosher salt and freshly ground black pepper

1 tablespoon extra-virgin olive oil

25–30 celery heart leaves, for garnish

Maldon sea salt, for garnish

Extra-virgin olive oil, for garnish

**Make the piquillo purée:** Place the peppers in the jar of a blender. Add the vinegar, olive oil, salt, and white pepper and put the lid on the blender. Blend until smooth. Add the xanthan gum, replace the lid, and turn the blender on low, gradually increasing the speed to high, until the mixture is emulsified. Set aside.

**Make the avocado relish:** In a nonreactive bowl, combine the avocado, piquillo peppers, and garlic. Stir to combine. Season with the salt and black pepper and add the olive oil, lemon juice, and basil. Toss gently to combine and set aside.

**Prepare the chorizo:** Cut the sausage lengthwise down the middle. Cut the sausage into thin strips.

Add the olive oil to a skillet over low heat. Add the chorizo and heat until the chorizo is warmed through and the sausage and oil turn orange. Set aside and keep warm.

**Prepare the octopus:** Heat a cast-iron skillet over high heat. Season the octopus with salt and pepper. Add the olive oil, and when it is hot, add the octopus and cook for 1½–2 minutes on each side. Lift each tentacle once to make sure it's coated in oil, and then don't disturb them again until it's time to flip them. You want a nice char on the exterior.

**To serve:** On each serving plate, spread a tablespoon of the piquillo purée. Arrange 2 tentacles per serving atop the purée, and scatter 3–4 strips of chorizo around the tentacles. Make 3 heaping 1-teaspoon piles of the avocado relish on each plate.

Garnish the relish and tentacles with celery leaves, a sprinkle of Maldon sea salt, and a drizzle of extra-virgin olive oil.

# SIDES

Exciting sides are crucial to any meal. They change up the flavors, textures, and rhythms of a meal, making dining more exciting and diverse than simply tucking into a big piece of rich protein. They can complement the main course or contrast it or both. We offer a bunch of sides with varying qualities of richness and texture—crispy from the fryer, fibrous from the vegetable world, and rich with cheesy goodness from the pasta universe.

First up in this chapter are the fried delicacies. *French fries* is so common a term that we forget what it means: The French created the fry. They call them *pommes frites*—fried potatoes. Either way, to put these crispy little morsels alongside a chewy steak was a genius move of textural contrast by the French. So I take fries very seriously. At Knife, we toss them with salsa verde, but you can also have them plain. And while you've got the oil hot, you might as well make some onion rings—another favorite of mine—or the irresistible avocado fries, which are so over the top you only need a few pieces.

Knife may be all about the meat, but I like my greens, and I like them clean. If you've got a vegetarian in the house and want to make the okra, feel free to leave the bacon out. (I also say this: Kale is a weed. I will always prefer collard greens, mustard greens, swiss chard, beet tops. I've never understood the obsession with kale.)

And, for the pièce de résistance, I give you the recipe for my version of mac and cheese, because it's the only recipe for this iconic side dish you'll ever need. Enjoy! ★

# SALSA VERDE FRENCH FRIES

Don't be afraid of making fries at home. They're not hard and often taste better than what you get at most restaurants, as you can make them as crispy as you like. If you do any frying at home, I recommend purchasing a designated fryer. They're cheap these days, and make frying easier, more accurate, and less sloppy.

For the crispiest (on the outside), creamiest (on the inside) fries, I recommend russet potatoes in this three-step process. When you're shopping for russets to make fries, pick up and weigh the potatoes in your hands and select the lightest ones. These will have less water, leading to a crispier fry. I like a somewhat thick, rustic cut from a squared-off potato; just make sure the thickness is as consistent as possible. There are plenty of methods for oven fries or single-cook fries, but I just find the results always better when they're blanched in oil, frozen, and then refried. It's a little extra work. But after the fries have been blanched and cooled down in the fridge, they can be easily bagged up and frozen. Then when you're ready to cook them, just dump some of the frozen potatoes straight into the hot oil. It makes a superior french fry.

SERVES: 2–4

2 large russet potatoes, scrubbed but not peeled

Vegetable oil for frying

Kosher salt

1½ heaping tablespoons salsa verde (see page 91)

Heat the oil in a deep fryer or in a heavy-bottomed pot to 250 degrees F. Line a rimmed baking sheet with paper towels.

Cut the ends off the potatoes and then trim the other sides to form a square. Slice the potatoes lengthwise ½ inch thick, and then the long way again into sticks ½ inch wide. Make the sticks as even as possible.

Fry the potatoes until they are pale gold and soft, 6–8 minutes. Remove the potatoes from the oil and drain on the paper towels. Separate the fries so they don't stick together. If you taste one now, it should taste almost like a baked potato. If you wish to freeze them to finish frying later, now would be the point to let them cool, put them in a plastic bag, put it in the freezer. It will keep just fine for weeks.

Raise the temperature of the oil to 375 degrees F. Fry the potatoes until crisp and golden brown outside and creamy inside, about 4–5 minutes. Sprinkle with salt.

Put the hot frites in a large bowl and top with the salsa verde. Toss the potatoes until the potatoes soak up all those herbs and oil. Who needs ketchup?

# ONION RINGS

I'm an onion ring fanatic, and I've tried so many in the world. It was either at Kraft Steak or BLT Steak in New York where I first had tempura onion rings, and they blew my mind. The test of a good onion ring is one that you can eat bite by bite without the piece of onion slithering out from inside the batter and slapping you in the face. This recipe will give you such majestic, perfectly flavored rings. It may sound like a production to make these at home, but it's not bad if you stay organized. My advice—use one designated hand to dredge the onions in the rice flour, and use the other hand to dip them in the batter. You'll stay much more clean and sane that way.

SERVES: 2

1 cup buttermilk

1 Spanish or large white onion

Vegetable or peanut oil, for frying

2 cups rice flour

2 teaspoons kosher salt, plus additional for seasoning

Tempura batter (see page 216), made with 1½ cups dry mix and 2¾ cups sparkling water

Pour the buttermilk into a nonreactive bowl. Slice the onions ½ inch thick and separate the rings; place the onion rings in the buttermilk and soak for 2–3 hours.

Fill a deep fryer or heavy-bottomed pot halfway with oil. Heat the oil to 375 degrees F.

In a bowl, combine the rice flour with the salt. Remove the onion rings from the buttermilk, a few at a time, and let the excess buttermilk drip off. Toss the onion rings in the rice flour until they are evenly coated with no clumps of rice flour.

Drop the onion rings in to the tempura batter. Bring the bowl to the deep fryer or pot.

Carefully drop the onion rings into the hot oil. Cook until they are golden brown, flipping them a couple of times so they cook evenly.

Remove the rings to a baking sheet lined with paper towels and season with a pinch of salt.

# AVOCADO FRIES

People marvel at our avocado fries, which are truly miraculous little greaseless, warm, creamy morsels served with a cooling but zesty chipotle mayonnaise. The inspiration came just after I moved to Texas, from a booth frying half avocados at the Texas State Fair. As soon as I saw them, I said to myself, *If I ever own a steakhouse, I will put avocado fries on the menu.*

Handle the ripe avocados as gently as possible when peeling so you can retain the most even wedge-shaped slices. Dredging the slices in rice flour before dunking them in tempura batter creates the protective structure that allows them to fry so well. When frying the avocado slices, don't drop them into the oil from high above, but take them directly to the oil with your hand before releasing them (and not burning your hand) so they don't sink to the bottom of the fryer and stick.

You'll know when the fries are ready by the color of the batter: a deep golden brown. Don't be afraid; you won't overcook them.

SERVES: 2

1 cup buttermilk

1 ripe avocado

Vegetable or peanut oil, for deep frying

2 cups rice flour

1 tablespoon kosher salt, plus additional for sprinkling

Tempura batter (see page 216), made with 1 ½ cups dry mix and 2¾ cups sparkling water

Pour the buttermilk into a bowl. Cut the avocado in half lengthwise and remove the pit. Peel the avocado and cut each half into 4 pieces. If they break, don't sweat it.

Soak the avocado pieces in the buttermilk for 30 minutes.

Fill a deep fryer or deep, heavy-bottomed pot halfway with oil. Heat the oil to 375 degrees F.

On a rimmed baking sheet, mix the rice flour with the kosher salt. Lift the avocado pieces from the buttermilk, letting the excess drain, and coat the pieces in the rice flour.

Place the avocado pieces into the tempura batter and bring the bowl to the deep fryer or pot. Carefully place the pieces, one at a time, into the hot oil.

Fry until the fries are a deep golden brown, turning them once or twice so they cook evenly. Remove the pieces to a pan lined with paper towels and sprinkle with salt.

# TEMPURA BATTER

If you're going to deep-fry something, I always recommend tempura as the batter. It's one of the millions of things about food that the Japanese have nailed. It's crisp, light, and greaseless—the perfect batter. We use it as a secondary layer to really create a great coating for our avocado fries and our onion rings. You can make this dried mixture and keep it fresh in the freezer or fridge, and as long as it stays dry, it keeps forever. You can use seltzer, club soda, or a mineral water like San Pellegrino for the batter. If you use club soda or mineral water, you may want to cut back on the salt a little.

YIELD: 8 CUPS DRY MIX

4 cups cake flour
4 cups all-purpose flour
2 tablespoons baking powder
3 tablespoons kosher salt
2¾ cups sparkling water

Sift or whisk together the cake flour, all-purpose flour, baking powder, and salt.

**To make the batter:** In a large bowl, whisk 1½ cups dry mix with the sparkling water. The batter should have the consistency of a crêpe batter or vegetable oil.

# JOHNNY MAC & CHEESE

I've been making this hedonistic version of mac and cheese for years, and it's still never been bested. This is unapologetically rich. So I'm not apologizing. It starts with a béchamel sauce, made with a blond roux—that's not the burned roux in gumbo. The theory behind the roux is that it's going to determine the consistency of your sauce, so if you want your sauce to be velvety and creamy, your roux had better be that way too.

The majority of the liquid is milk. There's a little cream for richness, but we don't need much because we use so much cheese. Heating the milk and cream separately from the other ingredients may seem like a pain, but it actually shortens the cooking time of the cheese sauce. You could add the milk and cream cold, but then you'd run the risk of a lumpy roux. I prefer Cabot Vermont sharp cheddar combined with a sharp New York cheddar. In classic French terms, when you stir the cheese into the béchamel, it becomes a Mornay sauce, minus the egg yolk.

Cook the macaroni until tender, not al dente. This is good old-fashioned American cooking, not Italian! This mac and cheese is great when served in individual small cast-iron pans or ramekins, after finishing in the oven.

SERVES: 6–8

4 slices bread, crusts removed

1 tablespoon plus ¼ teaspoon kosher salt

⅛ teaspoon freshly ground black pepper

2 tablespoons chopped parsley

1 pound (4 cups) elbow macaroni

3 cups whole milk

1 cup heavy cream

8 tablespoons butter, cut into chunks

¾ cup all-purpose flour

¼ teaspoon ground nutmeg

5 dashes green Tabasco

1½ cups plus 2 tablespoons shredded Vermont white cheddar

1½ cups plus 2 tablespoons shredded New York sharp cheddar

2 tablespoons 75/25 canola/olive oil blend (see page 88)

Crumbled cooked bacon, optional

Preheat the oven to 325 degrees F.

Place the bread on a baking sheet and toast in the oven until light golden brown. Let cool and then place in the bowl of a food processor and pulse to make bread crumbs. Add ¼ teaspoon of the salt, ⅛ teaspoon of the pepper, and the parsley and pulse once or twice to combine.

Raise the oven temperature to 350 degrees F.

Cook the macaroni according to the package directions until tender. Drain and keep warm.

(recipe continues)

Pour the milk and cream into a saucepan over medium heat. Heat just until you see bubbles forming around the edge of the pan; do not let the mixture boil. Keep warm.

Place the butter in a saucepan. Turn the heat to medium and melt the butter, stirring constantly. Don't let it brown. As it melts, the fat and milk solids will separate, and the water in the butter will start to boil. Now add the flour and stir until you have a smooth paste, or roux. Add the milk and cream, stirring constantly, until you have a velvety smooth mixture (a roux) with no lumps. Do not let the roux color.

Add the remaining 1 tablespoon salt, the nutmeg, and the green Tabasco. Stir.

Turn down the heat to low and add the cheeses. Add the elbow macaroni and gently stir until all the pasta is covered with sauce.

Spoon the mixture into individual serving dishes or a 3-quart casserole. Put the casserole(s) into the oven for 2–3 minutes or until you see the cheese start to darken.

Remove the mac and cheese. Sprinkle the bread crumbs evenly over the mac and cheese and drizzle with the oil. If you want to add some crumbled bacon, do it now. Put the casserole(s) back in the oven for another 2–3 minutes.

# VEGE-
TARIAN
COLLARD
GREENS

The Southern way of cooking collards usually
sees them smothered in bacon fat or stewed with
a ham hock. These are legitimately vegetarian.
By fully seasoning the cooking water, we provide
some of the external flavor for the greens that
meat usually would. You could add some sautéed
or caramelized onions to this, but I like it just
the way it is.

When you're reheating the greens, leave out
the butter if you're serving vegans or people who
can't eat dairy, subbing in olive oil instead.

SERVES: 4

2 large bunches collard greens, well washed

3 tablespoons plus 1 teaspoon kosher salt

1 Spanish onion

1 sprig thyme

4 fresh or dried bay leaves

1 tablespoon black peppercorns

1 clove garlic, halved

½ cup water

1 tablespoon butter or extra-virgin olive oil

¼ teaspoon freshly ground white pepper

Remove the stems from the collards by running
your knife down either side of the stem. Discard
the stems or feed them to your rabbit.

In a large pot, bring 5 quarts water to a boil
and add 3 tablespoons of the kosher salt. Peel
and quarter the onion and add it to the water.
Add the thyme, bay leaves, peppercorns, and
garlic and lower the heat under the pot. Let the
mixture simmer for 15–20 minutes.

Add the collard greens and cook, uncovered,
for 15–20 minutes, or until the leaves are
fork tender. Don't overcook them; you don't
want mushy greens. Put the cooked greens in
a colander and run them under cold water.
Squeeze out the excess water and set aside.

In a saucepan or skillet over medium-high heat,
add the water and butter. Add the collard greens
and stir. Taste and add up to a teaspoon of salt
and the white pepper. Continue stirring until
the greens are evenly heated through. Drain the
water from the pan, place the greens in a dish,
and serve.

# ROASTED OKRA, TOMATO & BACON

This fantastic side dish is credited to my mother-in-law, who made it to accompany a load of prime ribs I supplied one Christmas dinner. This side stole the show, though, so I in turn stole the side. Okra has the bad rap of being sticky or gooey, but we're going to avoid that by dry roasting it in the oven until it caramelizes and is golden brown around the edges. The sliminess comes from moisture in the vegetable, so by eliminating the water, we keep it nice and dry.

SERVES: 4

**5 slices applewood-smoked bacon**

**24–30 okra pods**

**½ teaspoon kosher salt**

**¼ teaspoon freshly ground black pepper**

**10 cherry or grape tomatoes, halved**

**2 tablespoons chopped chives**

**1 tablespoon imported sherry vinegar, like La Posada**

Preheat the oven to 375 degrees F.

Place the bacon in a skillet over medium heat and cook until it's crisp but not burned. Remove the bacon from the pan and coarsely chop it. Turn off the heat and reserve the bacon grease in the pan.

Trim the tops off the okra, halve the pods lengthwise, and place on a baking sheet. Season the okra with ¼ teaspoon of the salt and ⅛ teaspoon of the pepper and roast for 15 minutes, or until the okra is golden brown around the edges.

Add the bacon and okra to the pan with the bacon grease and turn the heat to medium. Toss together and cook for 2–3 minutes, stirring so the bacon doesn't burn. Add the tomatoes, chives, remaining ¼ teaspoon salt, and remaining ⅛ teaspoon pepper, and toss until the tomatoes are warmed through.

Stir in the sherry vinegar and serve.

# "CREAMED" SPINACH

It's the quintessential steakhouse side, but I wanted to take it to a new level, clean it up, and give a chef-driven, Frenchified touch. Traditionally, this dish becomes more about the cream than the spinach. I much prefer to honor the spinach with butter, in this case with the wonderfully useful and delicious form of "mounted" butter, beurre monté, that quickly and easily turns whole butter into a pliable sauce. This combination of tender spinach and sweet, tender roasted shallots is much lighter than the traditional version.

You don't want the spinach to absorb all the beurre monté; it should be lightly coated with the creamy sauce. If it dries out, lower the heat, add another tablespoon or two of the beurre monté, and heat until the sauce coats the spinach.

SERVES: 4

**4 shallots, unpeeled**

**½ teaspoon kosher salt, plus a pinch**

**Pinch freshly ground black pepper**

**½ teaspoon extra-virgin olive oil**

**2 (12-ounce) bags baby spinach, well washed and drained**

**1 cup beurre monté (see page 225)**

**½ teaspoon freshly ground white pepper**

**¼ teaspoon freshly grated nutmeg**

Preheat the oven to 325 degrees F.

Place the shallots in a square of foil. Season with a pinch each of salt and black pepper and pour the olive oil over all. Bring the opposite corners of the foil together in the center of the square and twist to make a package. It will resemble an oversized chocolate kiss. Place the package in an ovenproof pan and bake for 1¼ hours. Remove the pan from the oven, open the package, and let the shallots cool slightly. Cut the ends off the shallots and squeeze the shallots out of their skins onto a chopping board. Discard the skins and any tough parts and coarsely chop the shallots. Set aside.

Bring a pot of lightly salted water to a boil. Fill a bowl with ice water.

Blanch the spinach in the boiling water for 30–45 seconds; don't overcook. Remove the spinach with tongs or a slotted spoon to the ice water. Let it cool for a minute, then drain the spinach, place it in a clean kitchen towel, and wrap the towel around the spinach to form a ball. Squeeze out as much water as possible from the spinach and remove the ball of spinach to a cutting board. Cut into thirds.

In a sauté pan over medium-high heat, warm 1 cup of the beurre monté. Add the shallots, salt, the white pepper, and the nutmeg and stir. Fold in the spinach, lower the heat, and cook for 2–3 minutes; the spinach will absorb some of the beurre monté. The spinach should be hot with a creamy texture.

Serve immediately.

# BEURRE MONTÉ

A very useful thing to have around the kitchen, beurre monté is basically emulsified water and butter. I use it place of cream in a lot of my sauces because I think cream masks the flavors of other ingredients. The long-cooked shallots help keep the sauce from separating. I usually wind up using about 6 cups water. The sauce will keep, covered, in the refrigerator, for more than a week, or in the freezer indefinitely. If the sauce breaks when you reheat it, throw it back in the blender or use an immersion blender to re-emulsify it.

YIELD: 4 CUPS

8 large shallots, ends trimmed, thinly sliced
4 cups water, plus more if needed
1½ pounds unsalted butter, cut into chunks

In a large saucepan, combine the shallots and water over medium heat and bring to a simmer. Lower the heat and cook until the shallots are literally falling apart, 45–60 minutes. If you need to add more water as the shallots cook, do; in the end, you want as much water as shallots in the pot.

Put the shallots and remaining water in a blender. Holding the cover of the blender with a towel, blend, starting on the lowest speed and gradually increasing it to high until you have a smooth purée. With the blender running, add the butter, a little at a time, and blend until you have an opaque, creamy sauce that coats the back of a spoon.

# ONE DESSERT

Given that the focus of this book is meat and I never want to distract from that, I'm not going to delve deeply into dessert. But at the end of every nice meal, especially one at a steakhouse, it's nice to finish with a taste of sweet.

When it comes to a steak dinner or some other meat fest, my philosophy can be summed up like this: "You might as well have the chocolate!" After all, why hedge with a bowl of strawberries or a scoop of melon sorbet when, if you've made dinner from this book, you might have already been through bacon-crusted bone marrow, Caesar salad, a rib eye steak cooked Back to the Pan, and a side of mac and cheese? No, go for the chocolate. Indulge and enjoy in something decadent, refined, and pithy—a perfect close to a great meal. The recipe I present here is one of my favorites, the only chocolate dessert you'll need.

# CHOCOLATE COFFEE TART

This is a somewhat simplified version of one of our signature desserts. It may seem complicated, but the individual components are not difficult, and they can even be made ahead and assembled at the last minute.

Knife pastry chef Eric Cobb based the filling on an Italian *budino*—a rich, dense chocolate pudding, which contrasts with the tender tart shell, the cold, crunchy crystals of espresso granita, and satiny salty-sweet caramel sauce.

Use dark roast coffee beans, like French roast or espresso, for the custard. When you're making the salted caramel sauce, patience is a key ingredient. Take your time with each step of the process, or you'll wind up with burned clumps of sugar and have to start over again. But when it all comes together, this dessert is a stunner!

SERVES: 6

FOR THE ESPRESSO GRANITA:

½ cup sugar

3 cups warm water

3 ounces espresso

FOR THE CHOCOLATE TART SHELLS:

8 tablespoons unsalted butter

¼ cup plus 1½ teaspoons granulated sugar

1 ounce liquid eggs, like Egg Beaters, plus more if needed, or 1 large egg yolk, plus more if needed

½ teaspoon vanilla extract

1 cup plus 2 tablespoons cake flour, plus additional for dusting

¼ cup plus 1 tablespoon unsweetened cocoa powder

¾ teaspoon kosher salt

FOR THE COFFEE CHOCOLATE CUSTARD:

½ cup whole milk

¼ cup heavy cream

¼ vanilla bean

2 tablespoons whole coffee beans

1 large egg yolk

2 tablespoons plus ¾ teaspoon sugar

4 ounces (¼ pound) best-quality bittersweet chocolate 65–70 percent, like Valrhona Guanaja 70 percent, chopped

⅛ teaspoon smoked Maldon sea salt

FOR THE SALTED CARAMEL SAUCE:

¼ cup sugar

¼ vanilla bean, split lengthwise

¼ cup plus 1 tablespoon heavy cream

1 tablespoon butter

¾ teaspoon Maldon sea salt

**Make the espresso granita:** In a heatproof container, dissolve the sugar in the water. Add the espresso and stir to combine. Pour the mixture into an 8 × 8–inch cake pan and place the pan in the freezer. When the mixture is frozen, remove the pan from the freezer and scrape the surface with a fork to form crystals. If the mixture starts to melt, return the pan to the freezer until it freezes again. You may have to do this several times before you have a panful of crystals. Cover the pan and return it to the freezer until ready to use.

**Make the chocolate tart shells:** Preheat the oven to 350 degrees F. Lightly spray 6 muffin cups or mini-tart pans with cooking spray.

(recipe continues)

In the bowl of a stand mixer fitted with the paddle attachment, beat the butter and sugar on low speed until completely combined. Add the egg and the vanilla and mix on low until combined. In a small bowl, whisk together the cake flour, cocoa powder, and salt. Add half and mix on low until combined; then add the other half of the mixture and continue mixing until no streaks of flour show. The dough should hold together when you squeeze it; if it's dry and crumbly, add a little more liquid egg or egg yolk.

Turn the dough out onto a piece of plastic wrap and pat it into a circle about an inch thick. Wrap the dough and chill it in the refrigerator for at least an hour.

Remove the dough from the refrigerator. Dust a flat surface with cake flour and turn the dough onto the surface. Roll the dough into an 8 × 11–inch rectangle, ⅛ inch thick. You may need to add additional flour to keep the dough from sticking.

Cut 6 circles 4 inches in diameter and carefully fit them into the prepared muffin cups or tart pans. Place a cupcake paper in each tin or a piece of parchment paper in the tart pans and add enough pie weights or dried beans to cover the bottom.

Bake the tart shells for 4 minutes. Remove the pan from the oven, remove the liners and weights, and bake for another 4–5 minutes.

Place the pan or pans on a rack, and as soon as they are cool enough to handle, remove the tart shells and let them cool completely on a rack.

**Make the coffee chocolate custard:** In a medium saucepan, combine the milk, cream, vanilla bean, and coffee beans. Bring to a boil, turn off the heat, and steep the beans for 30 minutes. Strain the mixture, discard the beans, and return the milk/cream mixture to the pan. Return the pan to the burner and turn the heat to low; you want to see steam rising from the surface of the mixture. It's okay if small bubbles appear around the edge, but don't let the mixture boil.

In a small heatproof bowl, whisk the egg yolk and sugar until completely combined. Place the chopped chocolate in a large heatproof bowl.

Add a few tablespoons of the hot milk mixture to the eggs and whisk to combine. Add the egg mixture to the pan and cook, stirring constantly with a heatproof spatula, until the mixture thickens slightly and coats the back of the spatula.

Strain the hot egg/milk mixture over the chocolate. Add the salt and blend with an immersion blender until completely smooth.

Press a large piece of plastic wrap over the surface of the custard so it doesn't form a skin. Set aside and let cool to room temperature.

When the custard is cool, fill the tart shells evenly.

**Make the salted caramel sauce:** In a heavy-bottomed saucepan over medium-high heat, add the sugar. Stir the sugar constantly with a heatproof spatula, until it turns golden brown.

Add the vanilla bean and slowly add a tablespoon or two of the cream. Let the mixture bubble for a few seconds and then slowly add the remaining cream. Be careful; it will bubble up. Stir constantly until all the sugar has dissolved.

While continuing to stir, add the butter and salt and stir until dissolved. Remove the pan from the heat to cool slightly.

**To plate the dessert:** Lay out six plates. Put a tablespoon of the caramel sauce on each plate and smear it with the back of the spoon.

Place a filled tart shell in the middle of each smear. Scoop out a tablespoon of granita and place it at the side of the tart. Serve immediately.

# ACKNOWLEDGMENTS

This is my first book, and I can't say how much it means to me to see my thoughts on cooking represented on the printed page. It's both a thrill and a highly emotional experience, one that becomes only more poignant when I think about the many people who helped me get to this point.

First and foremost, I honor my mother, Eleanor, my grandmother Francis, and my aunt Anna. These were the women who showed me at an early age that cooking was important and made a difference in people's lives. They demonstrated the joys of being in the kitchen and provided the model of hard work that I would follow the rest of my life.

I think of Billy Thorne, the man who gave me an opportunity to work at Magic's and showed me the glamour in cooking for not just important people but for a real-life community. Then I think of Pierre and Francine Farkas, the duo who owned Club Pierre and who made my introduction to French food and the glories of Gallic cuisine.

Along my path in New York were my partners in 13 Barrow Street, guys who supported me fully at a time when I needed to be reinvented. To the great Gael Greene of *New York* magazine, for the being the one critic who really, truly got me—every time. Her praise has been a beacon for me throughout my entire career. Jim DeVine was instrumental in my evolution. The maître d' at the River Café, he both introduced me to Gael Greene and got me 13 Barrow Street.

So many great chefs along the way have made huge differences in how I think about food, cooking, my career, life. I love being a chef for many reasons, but the camaraderie and brotherhood I have with other chefs is one of the greatest feelings. So I bow to friends and colleagues like Rick Moonen, Eric Ripert, Scott Bryan, Tom Colicchio, Bobby Flay, Douglas Rodriguez—great chefs and food minds all. Anthony Bourdain, thanks for writing about me and understanding who I was. All these guys, despite their towering fame achievement, always believed that I could cook and always gave me time and attention when I needed it.

I thank the great Dean Fearing, Dallas legend, for creating the space that brought me to Dallas and making my landing a soft one. Bob Boulogne, Duncan Graham, and Shane Krige composed the corporate team who stood behind me during the remaking of the Mansion and deserve a lot of credit for enabling my success there. Brad Woy, I can say that ours is a love-hate relationship. But you gave me Spoon—my greatest restaurant achievement prior to Knife—and I'm eternally grateful.

There are many people that spurred the cooking and the awakening that led to Knife and this book. Michael O'Hanlon helped create the physical space and the opportunity for the existence of Knife. Adam Perry Lang and Mario Batali, thanks for teaching me about aging beef. Jason Schimmels and Bob McClaren of 44 Farms gave me raw product of the highest integrity so instrumental to Knife's success. And the same goes to all the guys at Creekstone and HeartBrand Beef. Josh Smith of Boston, a great friend who has taught me so much about charcuterie and kept Knife continually supplied with his genius products. George Stergios, my director of operations at Knife, who's taught me so much, but nothing more important than how to be a better businessman, a lesson so long in the learning. I thank all the cooks I've worked with at both Spoon and Knife, who supported me and made it possible, but especially Neil and Brent for their patience, dedication, and loyalty. It means so much.

I offer my great thanks to the team who helped create this book. David Hale Smith— good friend, gourmand, agent, raconteur; he had the vision for this. To Jordan for having the patience to listen to me and capture who I am. To Sydny Miner for her clarity and diligence in wading through the recipes. And to Kevin Marple for his fantastic eye.

And last but not least, I offer measureless gratitude and love to my wife, Tracy, my son, Ryder, and the entire Elliott family—my late father-in-law, Robert, my mother-in-law, Stephanie, Boots, Misty, D. L., Beverly. I didn't have family when I moved to Texas, and not only did they become my anchors, they introduced me to the world of Texas ranching. From them I learned the stark contrast between what we're doing at Knife and what had existed before in the history of Texas ranching. I was lucky enough to fall into this, but this family did all the hard work and laid the foundation of everything I've done.

And, finally, I call out to my daughter, Morgan, wherever you are.

# INDEX